Clear Grammar 2
Student Workbook

Clear Grammar 2 Student Workbook

More Activities for Spoken and Written Communication

Keith S. Folse, Ph.D.
M.A. TESOL Program, University of Central Florida, Orlando

Barbara Smith–Palinkas
ELI, University of South Florida

Elena Vestri Solomon
ESL, Hillsborough Community College

Donna M. Tortorella
ELI, University of South Florida

Ann Arbor

THE UNIVERSITY OF MICHIGAN PRESS

Contents

To the Teacher

Clear Grammar 2 Student Workbook is part of a multivolume series of grammar books for beginning to intermediate level students of English as a second or foreign language. Book 2 covers grammar points for upper-beginning nonnative speakers of English, including articles, *be going to,* irregular past tense, *how* questions, adverbs of frequency, object pronouns, *one* and *other,* possessive, comparison and superlative, modals, and problem words. This workbook may be used by students who are using the *Clear Grammar 2* textbook or any other upper-beginning grammar book. In addition, the workbook could be used by students in an upper-beginning conversation course so that they may practice written grammar to supplement the spoken practice in class.

The textbook for *Clear Grammar 2* contains grammar presentations using deductive and inductive approaches to accommodate the wide variety of learning styles that exist among language learners. In addition, the textbook contains an array of exercises and activities ranging from simple fill-in-the-blank exercises to original sentence creation to error identification and correction.

The exercises in the textbook have both written and speaking practice for the grammar points. The exercises for each of the grammar points in the textbook are sequenced from controlled (easy) to more open (challenging) activities. However, the exercises and activities in this workbook provide a different kind of practice. The exercises in this book attempt to simulate real language situations through the use of realia, sentence study, puzzles, and more difficult objective (TOEFL-like) exercises. Thus, the exercises in this workbook offer a good complement to the exercises available in the student textbook.

The exercises in *Clear Grammar 2 Student Workbook* follow a similar format to facilitate use by both the teacher and the student. Each of the thirteen units in this workbook offers these seven exercises:

Exercise 1.   Realia
Exercise 2.   Original Sentence Writing
Exercise 3.   Realia
Exercise 4.   Game, Puzzle, or Similar Activity
Exercise 5.   Dialogue and Conversation Practice
Exercise 6.   Sentence Study
Exercise 7.   TOEFL Review

Exercises 1 and 3 are called **Realia.** In these exercises, students will work with postcards, newspaper articles, advertisements for various products, and other kinds of "real" examples of the grammar point being practiced in a particular unit.

Exercise 2, **Original Sentence Writing,** requires students to write their own unique sentences from prompts. The prompts either include specific examples of the grammar point being practiced, or they elicit use of the grammar point. For example, in unit 3 on *be + going to* + VERB, the students are asked to write sentences with "is going to," whereas in Unit 2 on articles they are given various place-names as prompts, such as "Real Sea," which would then elicit the use of "the."

Exercise 4 is often some type of **game, puzzle,** or **similar activity.** Learners practice the grammar point while doing some challenging activity. Exercise 4 often consists of a crossword puzzle or word search activity.

In Exercise 5, students work with original **dialogues** and **conversations.** If they are asked to write original dialogues, general guidelines or parameters are given, such as the names of the two people in the dialogue as well as their relationship (e.g., two students, a witness and a police officer, a doctor and a patient). In addition, students are sometimes told exactly what problem to develop (and solve!) in the dialogue. For example, the directions for exercise 5 in unit 8 on *one* and *other* instruct the student to write a dialogue in which someone is shopping for a new car, is confused by the variety of models, and therefore has to ask a friend for assistance. When students are asked to read a dialogue, instead of writing their own, the dialogue helps learners by providing a clear example of how native speakers of English might use the grammar points in real conversation. This exercise provides practice not only in using the structures but also in listening for them in conversation. Thus, this exercise gives students practice in speaking and listening (as well as in writing and reading).

Exercise 6 is called **Sentence Study.** In this exercise, students must first read a given sentence or minidialogue that contains elements of the grammar points being studied in that particular unit. Next, students are to read four sentences and choose which one or ones are true based on the information in the original sentences. This exercise is a very important one because it not only helps learners sort out what the grammar point really means but also promotes critical thinking skills in English. In addition, it promotes reading skills in English through more rapid recognition of the given grammar structures.

Exercise 7 provides a **review** of the language points in the unit using objective questions of two types. Resembling questions found in the structure section of the Test of English as a Foreign Language (TOEFL), the questions in this exercise employ a multiple-choice format. There are two parts. In Part 1, there are eight questions that students are to complete with the correct answer by choosing among four answers provided. In Part 2, there are seven questions that contain four underlined words or phrases. In this part of the exercise, students are to choose the one underlined word or phrase that has a grammatical error in it. While students are not required to actually correct the error, teachers may find it more beneficial to ask students to do so.

Unit 1

Review of Book 1

Exercise 1. **Realia** Read the following postcard from Leslie to her sister Wanda. Underline the correct verb forms.

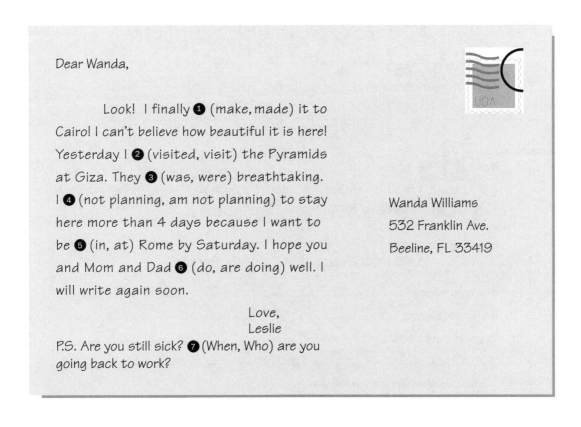

Dear Wanda,

Look! I finally **❶** (make, made) it to Cairo! I can't believe how beautiful it is here! Yesterday I **❷** (visited, visit) the Pyramids at Giza. They **❸** (was, were) breathtaking. I **❹** (not planning, am not planning) to stay here more than 4 days because I want to be **❺** (in, at) Rome by Saturday. I hope you and Mom and Dad **❻** (do, are doing) well. I will write again soon.

Love,
Leslie

P.S. Are you still sick? **❼** (When, Who) are you going back to work?

Wanda Williams
532 Franklin Ave.
Beeline, FL 33419

Exercise 2. **Original Sentence Writing** Read the following words and write sentences using those words in the blanks. Be sure to use the correct form of the verb. Pay attention to word order.

1. Why / Linda / be / not / in school today?

_____

2. Those / cookies / be / more expensive / than these / cookies.

_____

3. Jermaine / live / and study / in England / in 1998.

_____

4. Right now / Sally / watch / television / in her bedroom.

_____

5. The students / not have time / to do / their homework / last night.

_____

6. Why / you / leave the party / so early yesterday?

_____

7. My brother / not like / to play soccer, but / he love / to play baseball.

_____

8. You / from / Spain?

_____

Exercise 3.　**Realia** Imagine that you can interview any famous person, dead or alive. Prepare for this interview by filling in the missing information in the following form.

My Interview with a Famous Person

1. Interviewer's Name: _____

2. Interviewee's Name: _____

3. Your reason for choosing this interviewee: _____

_____

Five questions you want to ask this interviewee

1. _____

2. _____

3. _____

4. _____

5. _____

Exercise 4.   **Puzzle/Game** Read the clues for the crossword puzzle. Then fill in the answers in the puzzle.

Across

1. Lisa doesn't want *this* piece of cake; she wants _____ one.

3. the opposite of *peace*

6. Sugar is _____ .

8. I (come) _____ to class late yesterday morning.

9. A small insect that flies; it makes honey.

11. Bill comes from a large family. How many brothers _____ ? (3 words)

14. I only have _____ (2 words) money, so I can't go to the movies tonight.

16. My sister works _____ the National Bank of Wooden Hills.

Down

2. Right now we (review) _____ (2 words).

3. www = the world wide _____

4. the past tense of *eat*

5. What do you put in your tea to make it cold?

7. Yesterday I (wake) _____ up at 7:30 A.M.

10. _____ student in my class is studying grammar.

12. the opposite of *cold*

13. I _____ not hungry.

14. The plane arrived _____ 2:35 P.M.

15. the opposite of *big*

Across

18. a room in the house where you might keep your TV set

20. R_____ n_____ I am doing this crossword puzzle. (2 words)

21. not happy = _____happy

22. the present tense of *sang*

23. You add this small substance to bread to make it rise when you are making bread naturally.

Down

17. I have a _____ books. (= I don't have many books.)

18. Does Jillian have a car? Yes, she _____ .

19. a method of travel

20. the present tense of *ran*

Exercise 5. **Dialogue and Conversation Practice** Diana and Giovanni just met at the university library. Giovanni would like to know the following information about Diana. Write a dialogue with questions and answers using the words provided.

name	country	hobbies	major

Giovanni: _____

Diana: _____

Giovanni: _____

Diana: _____

Giovanni: _____

Diana: _____

Giovanni: _____

Diana: _____

Giovanni: _____

Diana: _____

Exercise 6. **Sentence Study** Read the beginning sentences. Then read the answer choices and put a check mark in front of **all of the sentences that are true** based on the beginning sentences. Remember that more than one answer is possible sometimes.

1. Sheila always watches TV.
   ___ a. Sheila watches TV regularly.
   ___ b. Sheila doesn't watch TV.
   ___ c. Sheila watches TV only on weekends.
   ___ d. She only watches TV with friends.

2. Frederic doesn't have any pets.
   ___ a. He has only one dog.
   ___ b. He has some fish.
   ___ c. He has no pets.
   ___ d. His dog died, but his cat is still alive.

3. I love pizza, and so does Sharon.
   ___ a. Sharon and I love pizza.
   ___ b. Sharon doesn't like pizza.
   ___ c. Sharon and I hate pizza.
   ___ d. We like cheese, tomatoes, and rice.

4. Today is Thursday, and our last exam was a big grammar test the day before yesterday.
   ___ a. The test was on Tuesday.
   ___ b. The test will be on Friday.
   ___ c. There was no test.
   ___ d. We didn't have a grammar test on Wednesday.

5. The cat is in the kitchen.
   ___ a. The cat is not running in the yard.
   ___ b. The cat is sleeping on the bed.
   ___ c. The cat is in the house.
   ___ d. The cat is playing with something.

6. I live at 1347 Fifty-sixth Street.
   ___ a. My house is next to Fifty-sixth Street.
   ___ b. My house is on Fifty-sixth Street.
   ___ c. I live next to Fifty-sixth Street.
   ___ d. I live on Fifty-sixth Street.

7. The plane left New York at 12:45 P.M. It's going to arrive in Vancouver at 3:00 P.M.
   ___ a. The plane is not at the New York airport now.
   ___ b. The plane is not at the Vancouver airport now.
   ___ c. The plane is leaving now.
   ___ d. The plane is going to leave soon.

8. Jonathan and Patricia went to the cinema last week.
   ___ a. They are at the cinema now.
   ___ b. They watched a movie.
   ___ c. They did not watch an action movie.
   ___ d. Both of them went to the cinema.

Exercise 7.   **TOEFL Review**

Part 1.   Completion. For items 1 through 8, circle the letter of the answer that best completes the statement or question.

1. ___ this beautiful picture?

   a. Did you drew

   b. Did you draw

   c. Drew you

   d. You draw

2. I don't have time to go to the picnic, but ___ .

   a. Bobby is

   b. Bobby won't

   c. Bobby does

   d. Bobby have

3. Can you give me ___ over there?

   a. pen

   b. a pen

   c. this pen

   d. that pen

4. Where ___?

   a. were you born

   b. did you born

   c. you born

   d. born you

5. Michelle only has ___ to study for the final exam.

   a. a few time

   b. a little time

   c. a time

   d. some times

6. I ___ an only child. I have three sisters.

   a. don't

   b. no am

   c. not am

   d. am not

7. Where ___ last night? I tried to call you, but there was no answer.

   a. you were

   b. were you

   c. you did

   d. did you

8. The electricity went out. We need ___ candles.

   a. a few

   b. a little

   c. any

   d. a

Part 2. Error Identification. For items 9 through 15, read each sentence carefully. Look at the underlined parts. Circle the letter that shows the incorrect part.

9. My mother <u>doesn't</u> live with me; she <u>lives</u> with <u>her</u> mother <u>on</u> Detroit.
            A   B   C   D

10. <u>How</u> long did you <u>lived</u> in Tokyo, <u>Japan</u>?
       A   B C   D

11. Every Sunday I <u>am playing</u> tennis <u>with</u> my <u>husband</u> and <u>my</u> friends.
                     A   B   C   D

12. <u>Where is my</u> new sweater? I <u>no</u> find it <u>in</u> my <u>closet</u>.
       A   B   C   D

13. <u>Tonight's</u> movie <u>start at</u> 7:30 <u>sharp</u>. I <u>don't want</u> to be late!
       A   B   C   D

14. It <u>is raining</u> almost every <u>day</u> <u>in</u> Louisiana <u>in</u> the summer.
          A   B C   D

15. Mary <u>doesn't like</u> <u>this</u> restaurant. She <u>is preferring</u> the <u>restaurant</u> downtown.
            A   B   C   D

Unit 2

Articles

Exercise 1. **Realia** Read the list of items below, and write *a, an,* or ∅ (no article) on each line.

> As any good baker knows, it's important to assemble everything you need before you begin baking. In order to make chocolate chip cookies, you will need
>
> 1. _____ electric mixer
> 2. _____ large mixing bowl
> 3. _____ measuring cups and spoons
> 4. _____ 2 cups of flour
> 5. _____ egg
> 6. _____ 1¼ cups of brown sugar
> 7. _____ tablespoon of vanilla

Exercise 2. **Original Sentence Writing** Read the following words and write sentences using those words in the blanks. Decide which words need articles and which articles you will use.

1. Nile / River / be / in / Egypt

_____

2. Berlin / be / new capital / of / Germany

_____

3. Kingdom of Saudi Arabia / be / on / Red Sea

_____

4. His cousins / live / in / Texas / Florida / California

_____

8

5. Nepalese guides / climb / Himalayan Mountains

_____

6. I / always stay / at / Hilton Hotel / in / New York

_____

7. She / study at / UCLA / in / California

_____

8. Hurricanes / form / in / Atlantic Ocean

_____

Exercise 3.   **Realia**   You are away from home on a business trip. It's your first time in this city. You decide to call your family to tell them where you are staying. Your family has never been to this city either. Look at the map and then fill in the blanks with *a, an, the,* or ∅.

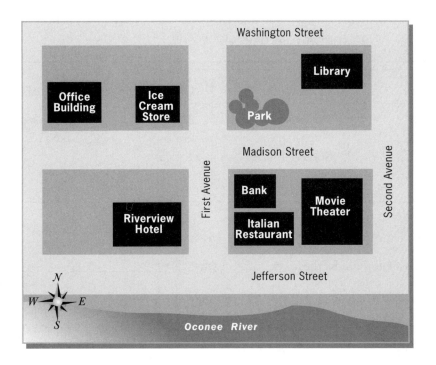

A: Hi! I made it. I'm staying at ❶ _____ hotel downtown. It's ❷ _____ Riverview Hotel on ❸ _____ Jefferson Street. Pardon? Yes, there is. In fact, I can see it from my room. It's called ❹ _____ Oconee River, I think.

B: Are you going to order room service for dinner?

A: No, room service is too expensive. I saw ❺ _____ Italian restaurant across the street from ❻ _____ hotel. I think I'll eat there tonight. There's ❼ _____ ice

cream store on ❽ _____ next block. Maybe I'll go there for dessert.

B: What about tomorrow? Is everything ready?

A: No! I still need to plan for tomorrow's meeting. Pardon me? Oh, ❾ _____ meet-

ing is at 9:00. It's around the corner, on ❿ _____ Madison Street, about two

blocks from ⓫ _____ hotel.

B: Are you having a good time?

A: For the most part, yes. Okay, well I need to go. I have to stop at ⓬ _____ ATM

first and get some money for dinner. I think I saw ⓭ _____ bank next to

⓮ _____ restaurant. I'll be home tomorrow night. Me, too! Bye!

───────

Exercise 4.   **Puzzle/Game** What's your geography IQ? Read the sentences, fill
in the blanks with words from the box, and underline the correct
articles. Check your answers with the answer key. Then look below
to determine your geography IQ.

Country	Continent	City	Body of Water
England	Africa	Abu Dhabi	Great Lakes
Qatar	Australia	Lisbon	Lake Geneva
Russia	South America	Tokyo	
United States			

1. (The, A) famous river in _____ is (the, a) Thames.

2. (The, Ø) Colombia is (the, a) country in (the, Ø) _____ .

3. (The, A) capital of (Ø, a) Japan is (the, Ø) _____ .

4. (The, Ø) Sahara is (the, a) desert in (the, Ø) northern _____ .

5. (The, Ø) Hawaii is (the, a) state in (the, Ø) _____ .

6. (The, Ø) Switzerland is home to (the, Ø) _____ .

7. (The, Ø) Ural Mountains in (the, Ø) _____ divide (the, Ø) Europe and Asia.

8. (The, A) country on (the, Ø) Persian Gulf is (the, Ø) _____ .

9. (The, Ø) _____ is (the, a) capital of (the, Ø) Portugal.

10. (The, Ø) _____ border (the, Ø) Canada and (the, Ø) United States.

11. (The, A) capital of (the, Ø) _____ is (the, Ø) Canberra.

12. (The, Ø) _____ is (a, the) capital of (the, Ø) United Arab Emirates.

How did you do?

Number Correct	Status
12–10	World traveler!
9–7	You've been around!
6–4	You're getting there!
3–0	Beginning traveler!

Exercise 5.   **Dialogue and Conversation Practice** Work with a partner. Look at the following diagram from an accident report filed by the police. Assume the roles of the witness and the police officer and finish discussing what happened.

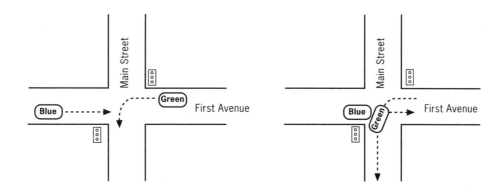

Facts

Car A = 1996 green Ford Mustang
Car B = 1998 blue Honda Prelude
Weather conditions = cloudy, raining
Time = Monday morning at 7:45 A.M.

Police officer: Are you a witness? Did you see what happened?
Witness: Yes, sir. I saw what happened. I was on the corner of First Avenue and Main Street when I saw a green Ford . . .

_____

_____

_____

_____

_____

_____

_____

_____

Exercise 6.   **Sentence Study** Read the beginning sentences. Then read the answer choices and put a check mark in front of **all of the sentences that are true** based on the beginning sentences. Remember that more than one answer is possible sometimes.

1. I need to use the phone in the kitchen.
   ___ a. There is only one phone in the kitchen.
   ___ b. There are two phones in the house.
   ___ c. The person doesn't know if there is a phone in the house.
   ___ d. The phone in the kitchen is not as good as the phone in the other room.

2. Hey, Don! It's 8:00, so it's time for the movie to start.
   ___ a. They are going to choose a movie to watch right now.
   ___ b. They are going to watch a movie.
   ___ c. They are going to choose a movie to watch after 8:00.
   ___ d. They went to the video store at 8:00.

3. He is on the winning baseball team.
   ___ a. He is a member of only one baseball team.
   ___ b. Only one baseball team won.
   ___ c. His team is the winner.
   ___ d. His team won.

4. I can't decide which movie to rent. The movie review says that the new Tommie Lee Jones movie is better than his last one.
   ___ a. Tommie Lee Jones is acting in his first movie.
   ___ b. There is a new movie starring Tommie Lee Jones.
   ___ c. There are two or more movies starring Tommie Lee Jones.
   ___ d. Both of the movies are expensive to rent.

5. They are moving to Florida, which is in the southern part of the United States.
   ___ a. Florida is in the southern part of the United States.
   ___ b. Florida is not in the northern part of the United States.
   ___ c. They are not living in Florida now.
   ___ d. They prefer to continue living in their current place.

6. *Bob:*   May, the computer is on. Did you use it?
   May: Yes, I did.
   Bob: Why did you use it? I mean, you hardly ever use the computer.
   May: I needed to finish a report for school.
   ___ a. May and Bob are talking about one computer, not two.
   ___ b. May and Bob are talking about the same computer.
   ___ c. May and Bob finished their reports for school.
   ___ d. May and Bob used the same computer to finish their reports for school.

7. A friend and I went to a restaurant on Cromly Avenue last weekend.
   ___ a. Everyone knows which restaurant they went to.
   ___ b. Everyone knows which friend went to the restaurant.
   ___ c. There is only one restaurant on Cromly Avenue.
   ___ d. There is a restaurant on Cromly Avenue.

8. The menu had prices ranging from $35.95 to $59.95.
   ___ a. The food costs $35.95 or $59.95 at the restaurant.
   ___ b. There are many menus to choose from at the restaurant.
   ___ c. There is only one menu at the restaurant.
   ___ d. There is no steak dinner for $29.95 at the restaurant.

Exercise 7.   **TOEFL Review**

Part 1.   Completion. For items 1 through 8, circle the letter of the answer that best completes the statement or question.

1. Last night I received ___ from my sister.

   a. one phone call

   b. the phone call

   c. a phone call

   d. phone call

2. She loves drinking coffee and reading ___ on Sunday morning.

   a. the paper

   b. a paper

   c. some paper

   d. paper

3. His favorite sport is ___ .

   a. a soccer

   b. soccer

   c. the soccer

   d. one soccer

4. I stayed up late last night to watch __ movie.

   a. the interesting

   b. a interesting

   c. one interesting

   d. an interesting

5. Where can I get __ for the table?

   a. fresh flowers

   b. the fresh flowers

   c. a fresh flowers

   d. the fresh flower

6. After thinking about it all night, he decided not to take __ they offered him.

   a. a new job

   b. one new job

   c. the new job

   d. an new job

7. I hear __ phone ringing. Can you get it for me?

   a. a

   b. the

   c. one

   d. Ø

8. Who was on the phone? Was it __ Nancy Young?

   a. Ø

   b. the

   c. a

   d. one

Part 2. Error Identification. For items 9 through 15, read each sentence carefully. Look at the underlined parts. Circle the letter that shows the incorrect part of the sentence.

9. <u>The</u> English is <u>a</u> difficult language for <u>some</u> people to learn in <u>school</u>.
      A   B   C   D

10. I want to take <u>a</u> steamboat down <u>a</u> Mississippi River <u>from</u> Wisconsin to <u>Louisiana</u>.
                     A   B   C   D

11. <u>The</u> students liked <u>the</u> movie starring <u>a</u> handsome actor <u>Leonardo DiCaprio</u>.
      A   B   C   D

12. Is this <u>a</u> book about <u>the</u> history of <u>the</u> United States that <u>John</u> gave you?
            A   B   C   D

13. I plan to go <u>on</u> vacation to <u>Arizona</u> next <u>year</u> to see <u>a</u> Grand Canyon.
               A   B   C   D

14. His favorite <u>food</u> is <u>the</u> pizza with <u>cheese</u> and <u>sausage</u>.
                  A   B   C   D

15. She and her friend have <u>the</u> same interests: <u>movies</u>, <u>music</u>, and <u>the books</u>.
                             A   B   C   D

Unit 3

Be + Going to + VERB

Exercise 1. **Realia** Read the announcement about planning for the future. Underline all the future tense verbs.

It's time to think ahead!
A public message brought to you by VEXAGON planning firm

Where are you going to live in 5 years?
What is your occupation going to be?
How many children are you going to have?
When are you going to retire from your job?
How often are you going to go on vacation?
How many countries are you going to visit?
How much money are you going to earn per year?
What kind of car are you going to drive?

If you cannot answer these questions, it is time to meet with us.
VEXAGON can help you plan for your future!

Call us now for a free consultation. The future is brighter than you think!

1-800-VEX-AGON

Exercise 2. **Original Sentence Writing** Read the following sentences that answer a question. Notice the underlined information. In the blanks, write questions that correspond to the underlined information. The first one has been done for you.

1. <u>Where are you going to go next weekend?</u>

   I'm going to go <u>to the beach</u> next weekend.

2. _____

   <u>Henrietta</u> is going to wear her new dress next Saturday.

16

3. _____

Karen and Billy are going to watch <u>the football game</u> tonight.

4. _____

My parents are going to go to Mexico <u>next month.</u>

5. _____

I'm not going to go with them <u>because I have to work.</u>

6. _____

I'm going to be with <u>my cousin</u> this weekend.

7. _____

My pet cat is going to stay <u>at my best friend's house</u> while I'm on vacation.

8. _____

Ricardo and Tom are going to visit <u>five</u> European countries in two weeks!

Exercise 3.   **Realia** Study the information on the Jones family's upcoming week. Write one sentence for each member of the family regarding his or her plans for the week.

Sunday	Monday	Tuesday	Wednesday	Thursday	Friday	Saturday
14 Nathan baseball game	15 Dee ballet recital 8 p.m.	16 Mom haircut	17 Dad seminar	18 Dog to the vet, noon	19 Tina science fair	20 Les bike show

1. <u>**Nathan is going to watch a baseball game on the 14th.**</u>

2. _____

3. _____

4. _____

5. _____

6. _____

7. _____

Exercise 4. `Puzzle/Game` The following puzzle has many words and phrases related to **time**. Find and circle eight words or phrases you can use to talk about time. The words are written horizontally and vertically.

```
S  N  A  L  W  A  Y  S  Q
Y  E  S  T  E  R  D  A  Y
Z  X  O  O  R  I  O  F  P
R  T  M  M  U  G  M  T  I
E  Y  E  O  W  H  V  E  C
T  E  T  R  G  T  W  R  S
A  A  I  R  B  N  S  O  T
L  R  M  O  Q  O  I  N  C
H  D  E  W  P  W  T  E  B
```

Exercise 5. `Dialogue and Conversation Practice` Nakisha and Ashley are talking after school. Nakisha wants to know about Ashley's plans for the weekend. Use the following *wh-* words to help you write a dialogue.

| What . . . ? | Where . . . ? | With whom . . . ? | Why . . . ? |

Nakisha: _____

Ashley: _____

Nakisha: _____

Ashley: _____

Nakisha: _____

Ashley: _____

Nakisha: _____

Ashley: _____

Exercise 6.   **Sentence Study** Read the beginning sentences. Then read the
answer choices and put a check mark in front of **all of the
sentences that are true** based on the beginning sentences.
Remember that more than one answer is possible sometimes.

1. I have to go out of town because my grandfather is in the hospital, so I'm not going to
   take the final exam with the rest of the students.
   ___ a. The exam was too difficult.
   ___ b. I was in the hospital.
   ___ c. I will not be in town.
   ___ d. I am going to see my grandfather.

2. It looks like it is going to rain.
   ___ a. Maybe it will rain.
   ___ b. It rained already.
   ___ c. It will not rain.
   ___ d. The rain looks really bad.

3. The company is going to move its main office to Miami.
   ___ a. The main office was always in Miami.
   ___ b. The main office will not be in Miami.
   ___ c. The main office is in New York City now.
   ___ d. The current main office is not in Miami.

4. Alice is going to move to Los Angeles for a better job than the one she has now.
   ___ a. Alice moved to Los Angeles.
   ___ b. Alice plans to move to a new place.
   ___ c. Alice will change jobs.
   ___ d. Alice is not living in Los Angeles now.

5. The plants are going to need water soon.
   ___ a. The plants are dead.
   ___ b. The plants are becoming dry.
   ___ c. The plants don't need water now.
   ___ d. The plants are in the water.

6. *Drew:*   How much time are you going to spend at the beach?
   Luke: Not too long. I can't go before 2, and I have to work at 6.
   ___ a. Drew is going to go to the beach.
   ___ b. Luke is going to spend a few hours at the beach.
   ___ c. This is Drew's second time at this beach.
   ___ d. This is Luke's first time at this beach.

7. *Ben:*   What time will the food be ready?

    Jen: The food's going to be ready at 5 P.M.

    ___ a. This conversation took place before 5 P.M.

    ___ b. They cannot eat the food at 4:30 P.M.

    ___ c. The salad will be ready before 5 P.M. but not the rest.

    ___ d. Ben asked Jen when the food was going to be ready.

8. My brothers are going to play in a soccer game tomorrow.

    ___ a. They usually play in a soccer game.

    ___ b. There is a soccer game tomorrow.

    ___ c. They are going to win the game.

    ___ d. My brothers will play soccer tomorrow.

Exercise 7.   **TOEFL Review**

Part 1.   Completion. For items 1 through 8, circle the letter of the answer that best completes the statement or question.

1. Do you know if ___ tomorrow?

    a. it going to rain

    b. it is going to rain

    c. rain

    d. will rain

2. ___ dinner tomorrow night?

    a. Where you

    b. Where are you going to eating

    c. Where are you going to eat

    d. Where you going to

3. ___ clean the house, and Gyuri is going to make dinner.

    a. I am going to

    b. I be going to

    c. I are going to

    d. I going to

4. How long is Joanna ___ in Texas?

    a. going

    b. going stay

    c. going to staying

    d. going to stay

5. Are the girls going to practice the piano this afternoon? Yes, ___ .

    a. they do

    b. they practice

    c. they are

    d. do

6. Peter and Rosanne ___ get married next year.

    a. going to

    b. be going to

    c. is going to

    d. are going to

7. Nance ___ come to graduation because she is sick.

    a. not going to

    b. isn't going to

    c. is going to

    d. not go to

8. I'm going to ___ one day.

    a. be pilot

    b. not be pilot

    c. be a pilot

    d. a pilot

Part 2. Error Identification. For items 9 through 15, read each sentence carefully. Look at the underlined parts. Circle the letter that shows the incorrect part of the sentence.

9. I cannot <u>come</u> <u>to</u> your house because I <u>going to</u> visit my grandmother <u>tonight</u>.
           A   B   C   D

10. Yvonne <u>isn't</u> going <u>to finish</u> school, but her <u>sister</u> Lorna <u>does</u>.
             A   B   C   D

11. <u>My</u> friends and I <u>are going to</u> <u>cooks</u> a big dinner <u>on</u> Saturday night.
   A   B   C   D

12. <u>The</u> new James Bond movie <u>is</u> going to <u>be very</u> successful, I <u>thinks</u>.
   A   B   C   D

13. <u>Last</u> week <u>we</u> are all going <u>to go</u> to <u>the</u> mountains.
   A   B   C   D

14. <u>It</u> is probably going <u>to be</u> a cold <u>winter</u> <u>last</u> year.
A   B   C   D

15. Next year we <u>went</u> to Las Vegas <u>for</u> the first time <u>in</u> our <u>lives</u>.
           A   B   C   D

Unit 4

Irregular Past Tense

Exercise 1. **Realia** The Jimenez family has just finished grocery shopping, but they have forgotten something very important. Read about their problem and fill in the blanks with the past tense of the verbs in parentheses.

WOW! Look at how much food we ❶ (buy) _____! Boy, it

sure ❷ (cost) _____ a lot of money. I ❸ (see) _____

"ice cream" on our shopping list, but I don't see it on this receipt.

_____ we ❹ (buy) _____ ice cream? I ❺ (go)

_____ to the wrong aisle. Who ❻ (get) _____ the

ice cream? No one? Do you mean we ❼ (forget) _____ to

buy ice cream? We **8** (spend) _____ all that money for

NOTHING!!!

Exercise 2. **Original Sentence Writing** Use the following words to write statements or questions in the past tense. Add capital letters and articles as needed.

example: dog / run / back home / ? **Did the dog run back home?**

1. parents / understand / child's question / ?

   _____

2. I / not catch / a cold last month / .

   _____

3. choir / sing / favorite Christmas song / .

   _____

4. Mrs. Jones / not speak with / phone company about the problem / ?

   _____

5. you / hold / your breath / .

   _____

6. brother / not break / his leg / .

   _____

7. your mother / make / dinner / ?

   _____

8. Mary / not write / several letters to her pen pal / ?

   _____

Exercise 3. **Realia** Study Sarah's schedule. Then write a complete sentence in the past tense to answer each question.

1. What did Sarah have to do on Sunday?

   _____

2. On Monday, did Sarah wake up at 5 or 6?

   _____

SUNDAY	free
MONDAY	wake up at 6 run for 1 hr.
	meet Joe for lunch
TUESDAY	meeting VP Sales 10 a.m.
	call car insurance co.
	pick up kids after school
WEDNESDAY	write proposal
	give to assistant to proofread
	leave work at 3
	go to library for research
THURSDAY	go to night class
FRIDAY	write final draft of proposal
	give proposal to boss at 2 p.m. meeting
	pick up suit at cleaners
	make dinner
SATURDAY	play golf
	go to surprise party for boss

3. Did Sarah meet Jim or Joe for lunch?

   _____

4. Did the president meet Sarah at the sales meeting?

   _____

5. Did Sarah write a procedure or a proposal?

   _____

6. At what time did Sarah leave work on Wednesday?

   _____

7. Where did she go on Thursday?

   _____

8. What did Sarah do with the proposal?

   _____

Exercise 4.   **Puzzle/Game** Read the clues for the crossword puzzle. Then fill in the answers in the puzzle. The verbs in parentheses need to be put in the past tense.

Across

1. The construction worker (hurt) _____ his back when he tried to pick up the concrete bricks.

3. Nancy (lose) _____ her car keys.

5. Something, known as a burden, that you carry or lift is called a _____ .

7. John (hit) _____ the ball and broke the window.

9. Mars is known as the _____ planet.

10. A baseball player needs a ball, a _____ , and a glove.

11. The opposite of *in* is _____ .

Down

1. I (hear) _____ the good news about Sam winning the prize.

2. Peter (take) _____ his son for his first haircut on Saturday.

3. Anyone can win the _____ . All you have to do is buy a ticket.

4. While daydreaming yesterday, I (think) _____ about summer vacations when I was a child.

5. Harry (leave) _____ milk out on the counter, and it got sour.

Across

12. The opposite of *on* is _____ .

13. Muhammed Ali was the heavyweight champion of the world. He (win) _____ many boxing matches.

15. The conductor (lead) _____ the orchestra in a very exciting concerto.

17. My wife (bet) _____ me that I could not stop smoking. Luckily for me, I won this bet.

20. The fifth day of the week is _____ .

24. Another day of the week beginning with *T* is _____ .

26. You can have either cake _____ ice cream.

27. A nickname for Daniel is _____ .

29. The opposite of sick is _____ .

30. The ninth month is _____ .

34. A short form for *puppy* is _____ .

36. I live _____ 202 Maple Street.

39. The teacher (speak) _____ to Karl about his bad behavior.

40. The opposite of *yes* is _____ .

41. Numbers are either odd or _____ .

42. I will be there _____ six o'clock.

43. The opposite of *stop* is _____ .

44. The train conductor (blow) _____ the whistle when he saw the horse on the tracks.

46. The opposite of *from* is _____ .

Down

6. The official (draw) _____ the lottery numbers at eleven o'clock last Saturday night.

8. The storyteller (tell) _____ the children a scary story.

14. The opposite of *always* is _____ .

15. Last week, Mary (let) _____ her children walk home from school alone.

16. To answer in the affirmative means to say _____ .

18. A round toy on a string that goes up and down is a _____ .

19. The opposite of *even* is _____ .

21. Johnny's mother (hide) _____ the candy so he wouldn't eat it all.

22. Paul was afraid of the dark, so he (run) _____ home every night before the sun set.

23. The opposite of *never* is _____ .

25. He was afraid there was a monster _____ his bed.

28. A popular American dessert is _____ pie.

31. It was raining yesterday, but the sun is shining _____ .

32. My cousin (build) _____ a new doghouse for his puppy.

33. By the time the bell (ring) _____ , the students were already in their seats.

Across

48. present tense of *lit*

50. You celebrate the time you were born on this day. _____ .

51. When I was finished, I (put) _____ the milk back in the refrigerator.

Down

34. A dark violet color is _____ .

35. My alarm (wake) _____ me up too early.

37. A hammer, a saw, and a screwdriver are all _____ .

38. Susan (go) _____ to Miami last week.

44. Something babies wear when they eat is called a _____ .

45. I (do) _____ my homework before I went to bed.

47. Last night was the first time Mary and Tom ever went _____ on a date.

49. The opposite of *down* is _____ .

Exercise 5. **Dialogue and Conversation Practice** Two women are window shopping at the mall. Fill in the dialogue using the past tense of the verbs in parentheses.

Betty: What _____ Bob (buy) _____ you for your birthday last year?

Vicki: Nothing.

Betty: He (not buy) _____ you anything? Why not?

Vicki: He (forget) _____ my birthday! What _____ Andy

(buy) _____ you?

Betty: He (make) _____ me a special card in which he (write)_____

"ILY."

Vicki: What _____ he (mean)_____ by that?

Betty: He (mean) _____ "I LOVE YOU."

Exercise 6.   **Sentence Study**   Read the beginning sentences. Then read the answer choices and put a check mark in front of **all of the sentences that are true** based on the beginning sentences. Remember that more than one answer is possible sometimes.

1. The contestant who stood the longest won the endurance test and the prize.
   ___ a. The contest is still going on.
   ___ b. The contest is over.
   ___ c. One person received a prize.
   ___ d. All the contestants sat down at the same time.

2. Harry bought his fiancée an expensive ring that cost over three thousand dollars.
   ___ a. Harry didn't buy anything.
   ___ b. Harry bought some jewelry for himself.
   ___ c. The ring cost too much money, and Harry couldn't afford it.
   ___ d. The ring wasn't cheap.

3. As I walked into the living room, I saw a beautiful picture on the wall. I asked Mrs. Roma, "Where did you get it?" She replied, "My son, Tony, drew that seascape."
   ___ a. Tony finished the picture.
   ___ b. Tony's mother helped him finish the picture.
   ___ c. Tony didn't draw the ocean.
   ___ d. Tony's mother hung his picture in her office.

4. Jack bought a large number of items at the grocery store.
   ___ a. Jack went to the supermarket.
   ___ b. Jack went to the pharmacy.
   ___ c. Jack probably purchased some food items.
   ___ d. It's possible that Jack purchased other things besides food.

5. Jeremy wore a black jacket to the reception at the new office last Sunday.
   ___ a. Jeremy has a black jacket on.
   ___ b. Jeremy had a black jacket on.
   ___ c. I really liked the jacket that Jeremy wore to the party.
   ___ d. I haven't seen Jeremy in quite a while.

6. You borrowed my writing book.
   ___ a. I lent you my book.
   ___ b. I returned your book.
   ___ c. You lent me your book.
   ___ d. I borrowed your book.

7. He came right home after he went to the store.
   ___ a. He came home first.
   ___ b. He went to the store second.
   ___ c. He came home second.
   ___ d. He went to the store first.

8. Jane didn't understand the lesson in class yesterday, but she finally got it when her
   roommate helped her last night.
   ___ a. Last night Jane understood the lesson.
   ___ b. Jane understands the lesson now.
   ___ c. Jane had difficulty comprehending the lesson in class.
   ___ d. Jane helped her roommate to understand the lesson better.

Exercise 7.   **TOEFL Review**

Part 1.   Completion. For items 1 through 8, circle the letter of the answer that best
             completes the statement.

1. Howard ___ his homework at seven and finished at ten o'clock.

   a. begin

   b. begun

   c. begins

   d. began

2. The child ___ the directions very well.

   a. understanded

   b. understand

   c. understood

   d. understod

3. I have no money left. I ___ too many things.

    a. bought

    b. baught

    c. buyed

    d. bot

4. The police officer ___ to give me the ticket.

    a. forgought

    b. forget

    c. forgotten

    d. forgot

5. She has bad luck because she ___ a mirror last week.

    a. broke

    b. breaked

    c. broken

    d. breaks

6. The cartoonist ___ a picture of his favorite character on his door.

    a. draw

    b. drawed

    c. drawn

    d. drew

7. He ___ home too late, so he missed the bus.

    a. leaved

    b. lived

    c. left

    d. leaves

8. They ___ a new house right next to mine.

    a. build

    b. builded

    c. bilt

    d. built

Part 2.   Error Identification. For items 9 through 15, read each sentence carefully. Look at the underlined parts. Circle the letter that shows the incorrect part.

9. Harry <u>didn't</u> <u>buy</u> the suit because it <u>costed</u> too <u>much</u> money.
        A   B   C   D

10. It <u>was</u> <u>raining</u> during the game, <u>so</u> she <u>brings</u> an umbrella.
      A   B   C   D

11. Peter <u>had</u> a cold last week. <u>Do</u> you <u>catch</u> it from <u>him</u>?
         A   B   C   D

12. <u>Didn't</u> you <u>understand</u> what <u>he</u> <u>said.</u>
      A   B   C D

13. <u>Does</u> you <u>begin</u> <u>your</u> homework <u>early</u>?
     A   B   C   D

14. We had a <u>great</u> time <u>at the</u> picnic. Why <u>don't</u> you come with <u>us</u>?
           A   B   C   D

15. Drake <u>drinked</u> so much <u>juice</u> that he <u>didn't have</u> room for <u>any</u> breakfast.
         A   B   C   D

Unit 5

How Questions

Exercise 1. **Realia** Read the following questionnaire about time management skills. Answer all the questions.

HOMEWORK MANAGEMENT SURVEY

1. How many classes are you taking this semester?

   _____

2. How many hours per week are you physically in class?

   _____

3. On average, how much homework do you have in one week?

   _____

4. How much time do you spend doing your homework per week?

   _____

5. How much extra studying do you do per week?

   _____

6. Do you have a job? If yes, how often do you work?

   _____

Exercise 2. **Original Sentence Writing** Read the following sentences that answer a question. Notice the underlined information. In the blanks, write questions that correspond to the underlined information.

1. _____

   My car is three years old.

2. _____

   I have three sisters.

3. _____

One foot is <u>12 inches long.</u>

4. _____

I watch television <u>every day.</u>

5. _____

Marcus is <u>6 feet tall.</u>

6. _____

I have <u>5 dollars</u> in my pocket.

7. _____

I work <u>8 hours</u> per day.

8. _____

My suitcase was <u>very</u> heavy!

Exercise 3.   **Realia** Joanna is looking for a job. Yesterday she had an interview with Datacamp Computer Systems. Read the interviewer's notes from that interview. Based on the notes, write down six questions that the interviewer probably asked Joanna.

Joanna Kearsey, U. Penn. grad.

- Studied at University of Pennsylvania for 3 years
- Had 2 part-time jobs during college
- Did computer training for 4 years
- Has no professional computer experience
- Received excellent grades in high school and college
- Gave 3 letters of recommendation

1. _____

2. _____

3. _____

4. _____

5. _____

6. _____

Exercise 4. **Puzzle/Game** Read the following questions and try to answer them. When you finish, add up your total score. The correct final number is 56.

1. How many sides does a hexagon have?   __ sides

2. How many total players can stay on a soccer field at one time?   __ players

3. How much time in years is equal to a "score"?   __ years

4. If a woman's only children are "quintuplets," how many kids does she have? __ kids

5. How many feet are in one yard?   __ feet

Total Number <u>56</u>

Exercise 5. **Dialogue and Conversation Practice** Freddie is sick. The doctor needs to know some information about Freddie's activities. Write a dialogue using at least four *how much/many* questions for the doctor to ask Freddie.

Doctor: _____

Freddie: _____

Doctor: _____

Freddie: _____

Doctor: _____

Freddie: _____

Doctor: _____

Freddie: _____

Doctor: _____

Freddie: _____

Doctor: _____

Freddie: _____

Exercise 6. **Sentence Study** Read the beginning questions. In numbers 1 through 4, put a check mark in front of **all of the sentences that are true** based on the beginning questions. In numbers 5 through 8, put a check mark in front of **all of the answers that are possible** in response to the questions. Remember that more than one answer is possible sometimes.

1. How tall is Billy?
   ___ a. I want to know his age.
   ___ b. I want to know his height.
   ___ c. I want to know his last name.
   ___ d. I want to know his location.

2. How many diplomas do you have?
   ___ a. I want to know about your education.
   ___ b. I want to know about your job.
   ___ c. I want to know about your family.
   ___ d. I want to know about your work experience.

3. How far is the bank?
   ___ a. I want to know the distance to the bank.
   ___ b. I want to know the name of the bank.
   ___ c. I want to know the size of the bank.
   ___ d. I want to know if the bank is near here or far from here.

4. How much homework did the teacher give us?
   ___ a. I want to know the assignment.
   ___ b. I need help doing the homework.
   ___ c. I already did the homework.
   ___ d. I want to know if we have a little or a lot of homework.

5. How long did you live in Rome?
   ___ a. 5 years.
   ___ b. 10 months.
   ___ c. Next year.
   ___ d. Until I was about 17 years old.

6. How long was the concert?
   ___ a. Yes, it was quite long.
   ___ b. There were about 45 people there.
   ___ c. Some parts of the concert were boring.
   ___ d. It lasted for about 45 minutes.

7. How big is your house?
   ___ a. It is approximately five years old.
   ___ b. It has six rooms.
   ___ c. It is downtown near the bank on Williams Avenue.
   ___ d. It's not as large as the house I lived in before.

8. How many times have you eaten chocolate coconut cookies?
   ___ a. About three or four.
   ___ b. About three or four cookies.
   ___ c. It only took me about two minutes because they were so delicious.
   ___ d. Never. I can't imagine what that combination would taste like!

Exercise 7.   **TOEFL Review**

Part 1. Completion. For items 1 through 8, circle the letter of the answer that best completes the question.

1. ___ students are in your class?

   a. How much

   b. How tall

   c. How many

   d. How well

2. ___ did you stay up last night?

   a. How late

   b. How many

   c. How happy

   d. How many times

3. ___ Billy stay in the post office?

   a. How long

   b. How long did

   c. How many times

   d. How much

4. ___ do you speak English?

 a. How many

 b. How many days

 c. How early

 d. How often

5. How much ___?

 a. money do you have

 b. sisters do you have

 c. grammar books do you have

 d. dollars do you have

6. How tall ___?

 a. the Empire State Building is

 b. is the Empire State Building

 c. the Empire State Building

 d. are the Empire State Building

7. ___ away is your country?

 a. How much

 b. How many distance

 c. How far

 d. How many

8. ___ make one dollar?

 a. How many pennies

 b. How much pennies

 c. How pennies

 d. Many pennies

Part 2. Error Identification. For items 9 through 15, read each sentence carefully. Look at the underlined parts. Circle the letter that shows the incorrect part.

9. How <u>much</u> classes <u>are</u> you taking <u>this</u> <u>semester</u>?
     A   B   C   D

10. <u>How</u> many <u>job</u> did you <u>have</u> before you came to <u>this</u> company?
    A   B   C   D

11. <u>How much</u> friends <u>do</u> you contact every <u>week</u> on the <u>phone</u>?
      A   B   C   D

12. <u>How friendly</u> <u>are</u> the <u>new</u> student in your chemistry <u>class</u>?
      A   B   C   D

13. <u>How old</u> <u>your car is</u>? It looks <u>new</u> to <u>me</u>.
      A   B   C   D

14. How <u>many</u> time <u>did</u> you <u>spend</u> in <u>the</u> military?
       A   B   C   D

15. How <u>much</u> times did <u>you</u> call me <u>last</u> night? I'm sorry I <u>wasn't</u> home.
       A   B   C   D

Unit 6
Adverbs of Frequency

Exercise 1. `Realia`

Part 1. Take this quiz and find out your health IQ. Read the sentences and circle the number that best describes how often you do the following. Follow the example.

example:	**Always**	**Usually**	**Sometimes**	**Seldom**	**Never**
I avoid tobacco.	⑤	4	3	2	1

	Always	**Usually**	**Sometimes**	**Seldom**	**Never**
1. I exercise.	5	4	3	2	1
2. I eat nutritious food.	5	4	3	2	1
3. I take time to relax.	5	4	3	2	1
4. I have a remedy for stress.	5	4	3	2	1
5. I spend time with family and friends.	5	4	3	2	1

Now, add up your score. How did you do?

Score	Health IQ
25–20	Congratulations! You know what to do to stay healthy!
19–16	Super! You're very knowledgeable!
15–11	Good start—you're on your way to learning more!
10– 5	Keep at it—it takes time to learn what to do!

Part 2. Work with a partner. Ask each other what you do to stay healthy and share how often you follow the good health habits listed above.

40

Exercise 2. ▮Original Sentence Writing▮ Look at Steve's calendar for a typical month. Study his activities and then write sentences using the words provided.

Sunday	Monday	Tuesday	Wednesday	Thursday	Friday	Saturday
Call Mom	Class	Work	Class	Work	Movies	Do laundry
Play soccer	Class	Call Mom	Class	Work	Movies	Work
Laundry	Class	Work	Class	Work; call Mom	Movies	Do laundry
Call Mom; play soccer	Class	Work	Class	Work	Movies	Do laundry

1. Fridays / go / movies

   _____

2. Thursdays / go / class

   _____

3. Sundays / call / his mom

   _____

4. Saturdays / work

   _____

5. Saturdays / do / laundry

   _____

6. Tuesdays / work

   _____

7. Sundays / play / soccer

   _____

8. Mondays and Wednesdays / go / class

   _____

Exercise 3. **Realia** Read this warning label from a household cleanser and underline the correct adverbs of frequency.

Caution!

❶ (Always, Rarely) use this cleanser in a well-ventilated room.

❷ (Sometimes, Never) combine this product with another cleaning agent. Combining products ❸ (usually, sometimes) results in toxic fumes. ❹ (Sometimes, Often) this product may stain your skin or clothing. If the cleanser should get on your skin or clothing, rinse the area with water immediately. One application of this product is ❺ (never, usually) enough to remove most stains. It ❻ (always, rarely) happens that the stain cannot be removed. Even old stains can ❼ (often, never) be removed. If you have questions about this product or its use, call **1-800-NEW-LOOK.**

Exercise 4. **Puzzle/Game**

Part 1. Test your search skills. Find and circle seven adverbs of frequency. The words are written horizontally, vertically, diagonally, forward, and backward.

S	E	M	I	T	E	M	O	S
T	Y	E	L	A	S	F	S	O
A	L	W	A	Y	T	O	E	M
L	L	I	R	E	A	B	L	P
W	A	S	N	P	L	I	D	E
A	U	X	K	E	U	R	O	M
Y	S	O	R	E	V	E	M	A
S	U	S	U	A	L	E	I	N
R	A	R	E	L	Y	N	R	T

Part 2.   Use some of the words you located in the search puzzle to complete the sentences below.

1. She _____ studies alone. She likes to study in a quiet room with no other

   people.

2. They _____ go to the movies. Last year they saw three movies.

3. I try to exercise regularly. I _____ go to the gym three or four times a week.

4. Bob and Laura are married. They take turns cooking. _____ Bob cooks, and

   _____ Laura cooks.

5. Willie is a vegetarian. That means he _____ eats meat.

Exercise 5.   **Dialogue and Conversation Practice** Work with a partner. Last week you applied for a new job and now have an appointment for an interview. Write interview questions and answers using the following words and phrases. Then practice asking and answering the questions with your partner.

Interviewer	*Interviewee*
1. how / dependable / you	always / time seldom / sick
2. problems / co-workers / last job	never always / get along / people
3. ever / work / late	sometimes / work / late usually / project due
4. attend / many meetings	boss / often / ask usually / write / minutes sometimes / lead meeting
5. comfortable / computers	always / last job
6. thank you / coming	welcome

Exercise 6. **Sentence Study** Read the beginning sentences. Then read the answer choices and put a check mark in front of **all of the sentences that are true** based on the beginning sentences. Remember that more than one answer is possible sometimes.

1. In Canada and the United States, many people retire at age 65.
   ___ a. In these two countries, people always retire at age 65.
   ___ b. In these two countries, people rarely retire at age 65.
   ___ c. In these two countries, people usually retire when they are 65.
   ___ d. In these two countries, people never retire when they are 70.

2. Melissa usually has only a salad for lunch.
   ___ a. Melissa eats a salad for lunch almost every day.
   ___ b. Melissa probably eats a salad for lunch two days a week.
   ___ c. Sometimes Melissa doesn't have a salad for lunch.
   ___ d. Melissa eats chicken or beef for lunch, but she usually eats a salad first.

3. Three years ago John started a full-time job as a computer programmer. At the beginning of every workday, he receives a sheet of instructions, and then he programs the computer to do what those instructions say. When he is finished, he sends his work to someone else via e-mail.
   ___ a. John usually works with people at his job.
   ___ b. John usually works with machines at his job.
   ___ c. John doesn't like to work with people at his job.
   ___ d. John worked at the same place last year.

4. My workday begins at 8:00 A.M. and ends at 5:00 P.M., but I stay until 8:00 P.M. at least three days a week to complete my projects.
   ___ a. I always stay late to finish my work.
   ___ b. I never stay late only one day a week.
   ___ c. I often stay after 5:00 to work on my projects.
   ___ d. Sometimes I stay at work late four or five days a week.

5. They seldom pay the rent late.
   ___ a. They don't usually pay the rent late.
   ___ b. They almost always pay the rent on time.
   ___ c. Sometimes they pay the rent on time.
   ___ d. Their rent is not very expensive.

6. I don't often drive over the speed limit.
   ___ a. I never drive faster than the speed limit.
   ___ b. Sometimes I drive faster than the speed limit.
   ___ c. I usually drive within the speed limit.
   ___ d. Sometimes I speed but not often.

7. When John goes home at night, he logs on to the Internet for a couple of hours.
   ___ a. John spends all of his free time on computers.
   ___ b. John spends some of his free time on computers.
   ___ c. John sometimes spends his free time on computers.
   ___ d. John does not know how to check e-mail or use the Web.

8. Some people don't ever go to the dentist.
   ___ a. Most people seldom visit the dentist.
   ___ b. Some people never visit the dentist.
   ___ c. Everyone rarely goes to the dentist.
   ___ d. Some people go to the dentist.

Exercise 7.   **TOEFL Review**

Part 1.   Completion. For items 1 through 8, circle the letter of the answer that best completes the statement or question.

1. They ___ late for work.

   a. sometimes are

   b. sometimes comes

   c. are coming sometimes

   d. are sometimes

2. She ___ lunch with her colleagues.

   a. doesn't never eat

   b. isn't never eating

   c. never eats

   d. eats never

3. We ___ more than three weeks in Florida on vacation.

   a. aren't usually spend

   b. don't spend usually

   c. usually aren't spending

   d. don't usually spend

4. Do you ___ books for pleasure?

   a. ever are reading

   b. ever read

   c. are ever reading

   d. ever reading

5. Where I live, the weather ___ cold.

   a. gets rarely

   b. doesn't get rarely

   c. rarely gets

   d. rarely doesn't get

6. How often ___ TV as a child?

   a. you did watch

   b. were you watching

   c. did you watch

   d. you watched

7. He ___ in his yard on Saturday.

   a. works always

   b. is always works

   c. always works

   d. always working

8. Luckily, I ___ headaches.

   a. am often have

   b. don't often have

   c. have often

   d. don't have often

Part 2.   Error Identification. For items 9 through 15, read each sentence carefully. Look at the underlined parts. Circle the letter that shows the incorrect part of the sentence.

9. Thomas usually wait for his friend after class.
         A   B   C   D

10. Always the weather is very hot in the southern part of Thailand during August.
        A   B   C   D

11. Theresa and her sister are ever happy with their grades.
                    A   B   C   D

12. Do they usually shops on the weekend?
     A   B   C   D

13. I never am on the phone for more than an hour at work.
        A   B   C   D

14. The children at the center didn't never receive the toys.
     A   B   C   D

15. How often do you talk with a friends back home?
         A   B   C   D

Unit 7
Object Pronouns

Exercise 1. **Realia** Fill in the blanks with the correct pronouns or possessive adjectives.

A: This is _____ toy! Give _____ to _____!

B: No, _____ isn't.

A: _____ found it on the playground right next to _____ backpack.

B: Just because _____ found _____ doesn't mean that _____ can keep _____ .

A: Yes, _____ does. Finders keepers, losers weepers!

Exercise 2. **Original Sentence Writing** Write a complete sentence using the correct form of a pronoun wherever there is a _____. You may have to change some word forms. Add capital letters as needed.

  example: He / give / _____ / the book (past)

  He gave me the book.

1. I / tell / _____ / to be quiet (past)

_____

2. eyeglasses / break / when the baby / throw / _____ / on the floor (past)

_____

3. for Mary's birthday / _____ sisters / buy / _____ / a watch (past)

_____

4. for Peter's birthday / _____ brothers / buy / _____ / a football (past)

_____

5. _____ mother / let / _____ / borrow / _____ car (past)

_____

6. _____ friends and _____ / have / similar interests (present)

_____

7. Michael / bring / _____ dog / to the veterinarian to give _____ a flea bath (past)

_____

Exercise 3. **Realia** Jamal is going to make a sandwich from the ingredients shown in the picture. Here is a description of how he plans to do it. Underline the correct word in parentheses.

Look at all this great stuff! I can make the sandwich of my dreams. Let's see. First, ❶ (I, my) think I'll put a slice of bread on the bottom. On top of ❷ (them, it), I'll put slices of meat and cheese. On top of ❸ (its, them) will go the tomatoes and lettuce. To bring out ❹ (their, they're) flavor, I'll add pickles and peppers. Now I'll have to start again with another slice of bread, and this time I'll reverse the order. That means that the pickles and peppers will come first, and on top of ❺ (them, it) will go the tomatoes and lettuce. Then I'll add another slice of bread. MY HERO!

Exercise 4.   **Puzzle/Game** This is a game called "What am I?" Pretend you are an object. Fill in the blanks with the correct pronouns to complete the clues. Then solve the riddle.

What am ❶ _____ ?
Part of ❷ _____ is round. This is the main part.
Sometimes this part is green, sometimes ❸ _____
is purple, and sometimes ❹ _____ is red.
Another part of me is long, brown or green, and
woodlike. Sometimes ❺ _____ will break if you
bend ❻ _____ . This part is called ❼ _____ stem. I grow on vines.
People in France grow ❽ _____ in vineyards. France processes ❾
_____ into fine beverages served in fancy restaurants.
What am ❿ _____ ?

Exercise 5. <mark>Dialogue and Conversation Practice</mark> A shopper is trying to buy a lamp at an outdoor market. Fill in the dialogue with the correct pronouns or possessive adjectives.

Customer: How much is this old lamp?

Owner: How much do _____ want to give _____?

Customer: _____'ll say ten dollars.

Owner: _____'s worth much more than that. Look at _____ beautiful color.

Customer: _____ asked _____ what _____ wanted to give _____, and that's what _____ want to pay. There is a man down the street who has one just like this. _____ am sure _____ will be interested in _____ price. Do _____ want _____ to give _____ the opportunity to sell _____ product?

Owner: _____ drive a hard bargain. Give _____ ten dollars and _____ is yours.

Exercise 6. **Sentence Study** Read the beginning sentences. Then read the answer choices and put a check mark in front of **all of the sentences that are true** based on the beginning sentences. Remember that more than one answer is possible sometimes.

1. I was cold, so Mary lent me her sweater.
   ___ a. Mary and I were cold.
   ___ b. The sweater belonged to Mary.
   ___ c. Mary borrowed my sweater, and she gave it back to me when I was cold.
   ___ d. I gave Mary my sweater.

2. The girls went to buy textbooks for their math, science, and art classes. They needed two books for each of their classes. They used their credit cards.
   ___ a. The girls didn't buy their books at the campus bookstore.
   ___ b. The girls didn't borrow money from their parents.
   ___ c. Each girl bought six books.
   ___ d. One girl bought more books than the other girl.

3. Because the weather was so rainy and cold, John's parents rented him a movie at the video store.
   ___ a. John rented a movie.
   ___ b. His parents rented a movie for him.
   ___ c. John went to the video store.
   ___ d. John rented his parents a movie.

4. Carlos gave Jane a ride home in his new Corvette.
   ___ a. Jane rode in his car.
   ___ b. The car belongs to him.
   ___ c. She is the driver.
   ___ d. He drove it.

5. Joe is looking for his CD. He thinks he lost it at the mall when he was there with his friends.
   ___ a. Joe got lost at the mall.
   ___ b. Joe's friends found his CD at the mall.
   ___ c. Joe lost his friends' CD.
   ___ d. Joe lost his own CD.

6. There are three children in the Beston family. John, who is 10 years old, is the middle child in his family. His brother, Mark, is 15. His sister, Joan, is 8.
   ___ a. John's birthday is before hers.
   ___ b. John's birthday is before his.
   ___ c. She is younger than both of them.
   ___ d. Mark is the oldest child.

7. Because the company had such a great year financially, the boss gave all of his workers a gift for their birthdays.
___ a. The workers received gifts.
___ b. The workers got gifts.
___ c. The boss received gifts.
___ d. The boss sold gifts.

8. I deposited it into my checking account.
___ a. I have a bank account.
___ b. I withdrew money from my account.
___ c. I have a savings account.
___ d. I added money to my checking account.

Exercise 7. **TOEFL Review**

Part 1. Completion. For items 1 through 8, circle the letter of the answer that best completes the statement.

1. Susan's hands were full, so she gave ___ her book to carry.
   a. she
   b. I
   c. me
   d. my

2. Steve couldn't control his dog, so he put ___ on a leash.
   a. them
   b. us
   c. he
   d. it

3. The florist found a nice pot for the plant and put ___ in the window.
   a. him
   b. them
   c. it
   d. me

4. I will give ___ the money after I get my check.

    a. me

    b. yours

    c. you

    d. your

5. Our car broke down, so the tow truck gave ___ a ride.

    a. him

    b. her

    c. me

    d. us

6. Jane called Peter to talk to ___ .

    a. him

    b. her

    c. me

    d. them

7. The pharmacist sold ___ the wrong prescription, so I brought it back.

    a. you

    b. my

    c. his

    d. me

8. The repair people gave ___ their estimates.

    a. they

    b. us

    c. she

    d. I

Part 2.   Error Identification. For items 9 through 15, read each sentence carefully. Look at the underlined parts. Circle the letter that shows the incorrect part.

9. I <u>played</u> tennis <u>with</u> Paul and <u>him</u> friends yesterday <u>afternoon</u>.
     A   B   C   D

10. Steve gave <u>his</u> extra pens to Mike and <u>I</u> before <u>yesterday's</u> big history <u>exam</u>.
            A   B   C   D

11. Loretta's <u>parents bought</u> a stereo for <u>her</u> for <u>his</u> <u>sixteenth</u> birthday.
            A   B   C   D

12. <u>We</u> <u>singed</u> "Happy Birthday" to <u>him</u> on <u>his special day</u>.
    A   B   C   D

13. Our parents <u>always have</u> taught <u>us</u> to <u>be</u> respectful to <u>older</u> people.
               A   B   C   D

14. Sheila bought <u>an</u> extremely old house, fixed <u>her</u> up, and then sold <u>it</u> for <u>a</u> nice profit.
             A   B   C   D

15. The new car <u>is</u> yours and mine. <u>This means</u> it <u>belongs</u> to both of <u>them</u> equally.
              A   B   C   D

Unit 8

One and *Other*

Exercise 1. **Realia** Read the following advertisement for headache medicine. Underline the following words: *it, other, the other, the others,* and *another.* Then answer the following question: When do you use *another,* and when do you use *other?*

PAIN-B-GONE

Do you get many headaches? If the answer is yes, we have a remedy for you! Introducing **PAIN-B-GONE** . . . the headache medicine that is different from all the others!

We at **PAIN-B-GONE** know that you have taken other headache medicine, but you're probably not happy with the results.

PAIN-B-GONE is special. Our unique formula includes other ingredients, such as natural herbs, to help calm and soothe you. That's right. Other tablets contain chemicals, but **PAIN-B-GONE** uses natural ingredients that will help you get relief from another headache.

Why spend another day in pain? Try **PAIN-B-GONE**.

After you try it, you will be so happy with the results!

You've tried the others; now give **PAIN-B-GONE** a try.

Call 1-800-PAIN-GON for a free sample!

Exercise 2. **Original Sentence Writing** Read the following words and write sentences using those words. Add missing words where they are necessary.

1. Lisa / have / two car. / One / be / yellow, / and other / be green.

   _____

2. I have / three sister. / Two of / my sister / be / doctors. / Other / be / dentist.

   _____

56

3. You / have / a pet? / No, / I not have / one.

_____

4. Shelly / want / other / glass of milk.

_____

5. My CD break / yesterday. / I / want to buy / other one.

_____

6. There are / two new / pen / on the table. I / will take / one, / and you / can take / other.

_____

7. You / want / other / piece of pizza?

_____

8. My mother / have / three puppies. / Two like to stay / inside, / and / other / like to stay / outside.

_____

Exercise 3.   **Realia**   Read the following letter from Lina to her best friend, Maddie. Underline the correct forms of the words in parentheses.

Dear Maddie,

How are you doing? I imagine you're busy. I'm very busy these days. I have three final exams this semester. ❶ (One, Another) is tomorrow in calculus class. I just don't understand ❷ (it, one). Most of my classmates understand everything, but ❸ (anothers, others) cannot understand the concepts. I talked to ❹ (other, another) friend in class, and he is going to try to help me. I have ❺ (another, others) exam on Wednesday, for my history class. The class was great, and I really enjoyed ❻ (it, one), but I'm scared about the final. There are so many names and dates I must remember! My last exam is biology. You know how much I love ❼ (one, it)! I'm not worried about this one, but the ❽ (others two, other two), wow!

Anyway, that's it for me… study, study, study. Please write back to me and let me know how you are!

Take care,
Lina

Exercise 4. **Puzzle/Game** April is cleaning her closet and checking what clothing she has. Write sentences about the clothing. Use *other, the other,* or *the others* in your sentences. Follow the examples.

April's Closet Inventory

5 Sweaters	3 Pairs of Jeans	4 Pairs of Shoes	6 Skirts	7 Shirts
1 green	1 pair of black jeans	1 pair of tennis shoes	1 denim skirt	2 short sleeved
2 blue	1 pair of blue jeans	1 pair of high heels	1 velvet skirt	2 sleeveless
1 orange	1 pair of white jeans	1 pair of boots	4 long skirts	3 long sleeved
1 black		1 pair of slippers		

1. (jeans) *One pair of jeans is black. The others are blue and white.*

2. (jeans) *One pair of jeans is blue. Another is white.*

3. (sweater) _____

4. (shoes) _____

5. (skirt) _____

6. (skirt) _____

7. (shirts) _____

8. (shirts) _____

9. (sweater) _____

Exercise 5. **Dialogue and Conversation Practice** Diane is helping Melissa shop for a new car. Melissa is very confused because there are so many cars to choose from. Write a dialogue in which Diane helps Melissa pick the best car. Use *other, another, the other,* and *another one.* Use the vocabulary list below to help you.

2-door	sedan	convertible	green	metallic	automatic

Diane: _____

Melissa: _____

Diane: _____

Melissa: _____

Diane: _____

Melissa: _____

Diane: _____

Melissa: _____

Diane: _____

Melissa: _____

Exercise 6.   **Sentence Study**   Read the beginning sentences. Then read the answer choices and put a check mark in front of **all of the sentences that are true** based on the beginning sentences. Remember that more than one answer is possible sometimes.

1. When Jim finishes this book, he wants to read another book.
   ___ a. He has one book now.
   ___ b. He will start a new book when he finishes this book.
   ___ c. He works in a library.
   ___ d. His job is to read books and process information.

2. I will telephone ten classmates, and you can call the others.
   ___ a. There is a total of 11 classmates.
   ___ b. There is a total of 10 classmates.
   ___ c. There are more than 10 classmates.
   ___ d. There are not more than 14 classmates.

3. The other students are at the library.
   ___ a. Some students are not at the library.
   ___ b. All the students are at the library.
   ___ c. The library is closed.
   ___ d. Some students are at the library.

4. Irene will write another poem tomorrow.
   ___ a. This is her first time writing a poem.
   ___ b. Irene wrote a poem in the past.
   ___ c. Irene does not like to write poems.
   ___ d. The topics of the poems are different.

5. Larry's Ford Taurus is not running so well now, and his other car is in the shop.
   ___ a. Larry has one car.
   ___ b. Larry doesn't have a car in the shop.
   ___ c. Larry has two cars.
   ___ d. Both of Larry's cars are in the shop.

6. My other dictionary is in my backpack.
   ___ a. I have only two dictionaries.
   ___ b. I have only three dictionaries.
   ___ c. I have more than one dictionary.
   ___ d. I only have one dictionary.

7. Are you the only student in your class from Mexico? No, there are others.
   ___ a. Two students are from Mexico.
   ___ b. One student is from Mexico.
   ___ c. More than two students are from Mexico.
   ___ d. Most of the students in my class are from Mexico.

8. Lucille is going to have another baby soon.
   ___ a. This will be her first baby.
   ___ b. This will not be her first baby.
   ___ c. Lucille is pregnant.
   ___ d. Lucille is already a mother.

Exercise 7.   **TOEFL Review**

Part 1.   Completion. For items 1 through 8, circle the letter of the answer that best completes the statement or question.

1. Some people enjoy jogging, but ___ .
   a. others enjoy tennis
   b. other enjoy tennis
   c. another enjoys tennis
   d. the other enjoys tennis

2. Would you like ___ ?
   a. other cup of tea
   b. another teas
   c. another cup of tea
   d. others cup of teas

3. Sally wants to have more children, but she does not have enough money to raise ___ .

    a. one

    b. it

    c. them

    d. one other

4. Did you talk to ___ in the class?

    a. others students

    b. another students

    c. one students

    d. the other students

5. I'm taking four classes this semester; two are easy, but ___ are difficult.

    a. the other one

    b. the other ones

    c. anothers ones

    d. another one

6. I saw the new horror movie last night, but I didn't enjoy ___ .

    a. it

    b. one

    c. very much

    d. them

7. Karen has two sisters. ___ lives in California, and the other lives in New York.

    a. She

    b. One

    c. It

    d. Another

8. Rock and roll and hip-hop are two examples of music types. Opera is ___ .

   a. another

   b. other

   c. the other

   d. others type

Part 2.   Error Identification. For items 9 through 15, read each sentence carefully. Look at the underlined parts. Circle the letter that shows the incorrect part.

9. Yesterday I <u>ate</u> at the new Mexican <u>restaurant</u>. Tomorrow <u>I'll</u> go to <u>other</u> restaurant.
          A   B   C   D

10. <u>Six</u> of my <u>classmates</u> are male. <u>The</u> others <u>is</u> female.
    A   B   C   D

11. <u>Do</u> you want to <u>try</u> another <u>exercises</u> in this <u>book</u>?
    A   B   C   D

12. <u>One</u> example of <u>an</u> article is "the." <u>Other</u> example <u>is</u> "a."
    A   B   C   D

13. Today <u>the</u> weather <u>is</u> warm. <u>All</u> the <u>another</u> were cold.
        A   B   C   D

14. Let's go to <u>other</u> store. I <u>really</u> don't like <u>anything</u> in this <u>one</u>.
           A   B   C   D

15. <u>Do</u> you have <u>time</u> for <u>anothers</u> cup of tea before you <u>leave</u>?
    A   B   C   D

Unit 9

Possessive

Exercise 1. **Realia** Read the following story about a lost dog. Then fill in the blanks with the correct possessive forms. Sometimes you will only need to add a word ending.

LOST AND FOUND

Whose dog is this?

LOST AND FOUND

This dog is about six months old. ❶ _____ eyes are brown, and ❷ _____ hair is long and brown. The dog was wearing a blue and red collar. However, the buckle on ❸ _____ collar broke.

❹ _____ identification tag was missing, so

❺ _____ name is unknown. A little girl who lives on Maple Street said it looks familiar. She said it wasn't ❻ _____ dog. It looks a lot like the Jones family ❼ _____ dog, Lucky. The pet agency has contacted every Jones family in the Maple Street area. There has been only one response, and a member of ❽ _____ family will be here shortly. Look at that ❾ dog _____ tail wag. This must be one of the Joneses. What a lucky dog!

Exercise 2. **Original Sentence Writing** Write complete sentences using the given words to show possession.

example: ears / cat

    <u>My cat's ears are short and white.</u>

1. pencils / girls

_____

2. airport / city

_____

3. arm / chair

_____

4. the thickness / book

_____

5. news / yesterday

_____

6. sandwich / me

_____

7. price / stock

_____

8. prime minister / Britain

_____

Exercise 3. **Realia** Read the following statements. Then write the correct possessive forms for the items mentioned in the sentences.

example: Mama bought a new dress. **Mama's new dress**

1. Debbie has a school dress.   _____

2. The baby has a new jumpsuit.   _____

3. The Charles family has a new towel.   _____

4. The nightgown belongs to Mama.   _____

5. Dad wears old jeans.   _____

6. Both apartments share the clothesline.   _____

Exercise 4.   **Puzzle/Game** Try to solve the riddle.

IT'S ALL RELATIVE

Your brother's great-aunt's only sister.

_____

Your great great grandfather's only grandson.

_____

Put these two together. How are they related to you?

_____

Exercise 5.   **Dialogue and Conversation Practice** Bonnie and Clyde are taking a trip. Fill in the dialogue with possessives. Sometimes you will only need to add a word ending.

Bonnie: Where are you taking me, Clyde?

Clyde: We're going to the Bank _____ Boston. I hear Boston _____ weather this

time _____ year is really great.

Bonnie: Whose car are we going to use?

Clyde: I borrowed a car from my friend; it's Al Carphone_____ .

Bonnie: I didn't know the two of you were friends. When do we have to return _____

car?

Clyde: It's _____ decision—when I feel like it. And I may never feel like it.

Bonnie: The mark _____ a true friend!

Exercise 6. **Sentence Study** Read the beginning sentences. Then read the answer choices and put a check mark in front of **all of the sentences that are true** based on the beginning sentences. Remember that more than one answer is possible sometimes.

1. Frank asked, "Where's my dictionary? I left it on my desk."
   ___ a. Frank owns a dictionary and a desk.
   ___ b. Someone took Frank's dictionary.
   ___ c. Someone took Frank's desk.
   ___ d. Frank has to buy a new desk.

2. Both Susan and her sister Suzanne have the same color blue eyes.
   ___ a. Susan's eyes are blue.
   ___ b. Suzanne's eyes aren't blue.
   ___ c. Most people in their family have brown eyes.
   ___ d. Neither Susan's nor Suzanne's eyes are brown.

3. Peter stuck his gum on the back of my chair, which actually belongs to the Francis family.
   ___ a. The gum is Peter's.
   ___ b. The chair is mine.
   ___ c. The back of the chair is Peter's.
   ___ d. This is the chair.

4. John hid his toy car in a box so Harry couldn't find it.
   ___ a. John had a toy car.
   ___ b. The box had a car in it.
   ___ c. The box belonged to Harry.
   ___ d. Harry had a toy car.

5. Yesterday's newspaper was thrown into the trash can, so I asked Mary if I could borrow hers.
   ___ a. The newspaper that Mary gave me belonged to her.
   ___ b. Someone put yesterday's newspaper in the garbage can.
   ___ c. Mary borrowed my newspaper.
   ___ d. Mary's newspaper was thrown away.

6. Victor's name and that of his hometown both start with the same letter.

    __ a. The beginning sound of the name of Victor's hometown is just like that of his name.

    __ b. Victor's town starts with a "V."

    __ c. He may live in Virginia Beach.

    __ d. "V" is the beginning letter of Victor's hometown.

7. Of all of the students in Mr. Simpson's French class, Carla and Leticia are the best.

    __ a. Mr. Simpson's class studies a foreign language.

    __ b. Carla and Leticia are the only students in Mr. Simpson's class.

    __ c. Mr. Simpson is French.

    __ d. The class is made up of students from France.

8. My son's morning job is to walk our neighbors' dog.

    __ a. The dog belongs to my son.

    __ b. My son belongs to my neighbors.

    __ c. My son has a job.

    __ d. The dog belongs to me.

Exercise 7.   **TOEFL Review**

Part 1.   Completion. For items 1 through 8, circle the letter of the answer that best completes the statement.

1. __ hands were dirty from working on his car.

   a. Philips'

   b. The hands of Philip

   c. Philip's

   d. Philips

2. The baby broke the __ .

   a. handle of the cup.

   b. the cup's handle

   c. the cups handles

   d. the cups handle

3. ___ was in my wedding party.

    a. The sister of Harry

    b. The sister's Harry

    c. Harrys' sister

    d. Harry's sister

4. My mother's brother lost ___ watch the other day.

    a. his

    b. he

    c. us

    d. them

5. ___ was too bright for the print to show up.

    a. Papers' color

    b. Paper's color

    c. The paper of the color

    d. The color of the paper

6. ___ is 69 West Street.

    a. My house's address

    b. The address of my house

    c. My houses' address

    d. The address'

7. ___ is my uncle.

    a. The brother of my father

    b. The father of my brother

    c. My brother's father

    d. My father's brother

8. __ broke during the accident.

    a. The car's steering wheel

    b. The cars' steering wheel

    c. The steering wheel of the cars'

    d. The steering wheel of the car

Part 2. Error Identification. For items 9 through 15, read each sentence carefully. Look at the underlined parts. Circle the letter that shows the incorrect part.

9. The <u>color of</u> <u>Ruth's</u> hair is bright red. <u>Its</u> unique; no one else's hair looks like <u>hers</u>.
       A   B   C   D

10. Henry <u>lost</u> a <u>day</u> pay because <u>his</u> car wouldn't <u>start</u>.
           A   B   C   D

11. <u>My</u> mother <u>sent me</u> to the store, but when I <u>got</u> there, I couldn't remember the
   A   B   C

    <u>ice cream's name</u>.
         D

12. The <u>door's hinge</u> was <u>broken</u>, so we <u>fixed</u> it before <u>we went</u> on vacation.
          A   B   C   D

13. Our <u>family's</u> home has been painted <u>white and gray</u> ever since I can remember. <u>It's</u>
       A   B   C

    the only one on the block with those colors, and <u>thats</u> what makes it unique.
                                                  D

14. <u>Rick's</u> <u>sister's</u> husband painted <u>his</u> car blue, which is the same as <u>their house's color</u>.
    A   B   C   D

15. Whose gloves <u>is these</u>? <u>Mine</u> are the purple <u>ones</u>. <u>Sarah's</u> are the green ones.
                A   B   C   D

Unit 10

Comparative and Superlative

Exercise 1. **Realia** Read the advertisement for "Vit-a-lot" and fill in the blanks with the comparative forms for the words given.

New! Miracle Vitamin Discovered!

Look old? Want to look ❶ (young) _____? Feel tired?
Want to feel ❷ (energetic) _____? Hair dull?
Want it ❸ (shiny) _____?
Then try our new miracle vitamin! Just one Vit-a-lot a day for the next 30 days
will help you feel and look ❹ (good) _____. Taking Vit-a-lot is ❺ (easy)
_____ and ❻ (fast) _____ than exercising.

Vit-a-lot is ❼ (expensive) _____ than regular vitamins,
but using it will make you a lot ❽ (happy) _____!
Order your supply today!

Exercise 2. **Original Sentence Writing** Study the information below. Write one sentence making a comparison for two of the words or phrases. Write a second sentence making a comparison for all three of the words or phrases. Use the adjectives provided to make your comparisons.

example: Texas—92 degrees   Wisconsin—82 degrees   Montana—67 degrees
hot / cold

Wisconsin is hotter than Montana in the summer.

In the summer, Texas is the hottest of the three states.

70

1. Jane—23 years old   Lorraine—18 years old   Melissa—35 years old
   young / old

_____

_____

2. Bob—5'10" tall   Tom—5'9½" tall   Nick—5'8" tall
   tall / short

_____

_____

3. English   history   physics
   easy / difficult

_____

_____

4. jet   plane   glider
   noisy / quiet

_____

_____

5. flying   sailing   motorcycling
   safe / dangerous

_____

_____

6. skydiving   stamp collecting   in-line skating
   boring / exciting

_____

_____

7. a cold   a headache   the flu
   good / bad

_____

_____

8. computer   typewriter   paper and pencil
   efficient / inefficient

_____

_____

Exercise 3. **Realia** Read the travel brochure below and fill in the blanks with the correct comparative or superlative forms of the adjectives given.

Come to Florida for your next vacation. Florida, where the sun is ❶ (warm) _____

and the water is ❷ (blue)_____ than anywhere else! Rent a car while you're here. Among

all the other southern states, rates in Florida are the ❸ (low) _____. Enjoy fine dining in

any of our restaurants. The seafood here is the ❹ (delicious) _____ found anywhere

along the southeastern coast. Take a ride on a boat and see the dolphins. Beaches in the other

states are ❺ (crowd) _____ than here in Florida. The sunsets are ❻ (beautiful)

_____ from our shores than anyplace else you have been. Send in the postcard

on the back of this brochure, and we'll send you more information. Call us, and you'll receive

the information even ❼ (fast) _____. Then you can also start packing ❽ (soon)

_____ for your Florida getaway vacation. Call 1-800-FLORIDA today!

Exercise 4. **Puzzle/Game** Fill in the blanks with the correct superlatives. Use the words in the box below. Then match the description with the correct noun by drawing a line from the description on the left to the noun on the right.

high	long	small	far
large	old	busy	populated

1. the _____ river   a. Pluto

2. the _____ mountain   b. People's Republic of China

3. the _____ part of an element   c. Atlanta

4. the _____ planet from the sun   d. St. Augustine

5. the _____ mammal   e. Mount Everest

6. the _____ city in the U.S.   f. atom

7. the _____ airport in the U.S.   g. Nile

8. the _____ country in the world   h. whale

Exercise 5.   **Dialogue and Conversation Practice**   Work with a partner. James and Mary Ann Bowers are buying a home. They are trying to decide between two houses. You and your partner will write a conversation between James and Mary using the following facts. Use the adjectives and adverbs listed below to compare the two houses. End your conversation by making a decision.

| far | big | old | expensive | quiet | beautiful |

	House 1	*House 2*
Location	in a beautiful neighborhood	near a noisy highway
Distance	1 mile from work	6 miles from work
Size	1,500 square feet	1,800 square feet
Year built	1980	1990
Taxes	$2,300/year	$2,100/year
Price	$92,500	$103,000

_____

_____

_____

_____

_____

_____

_____

_____

_____

_____

_____

Exercise 6.   **Sentence Study** Read the beginning sentences. Then read the answer choices and put a check mark in front of **all of the sentences that are true** based on the beginning sentences. Remember that more than one answer is possible sometimes.

1. One of the most famous women pilots of the U.S. was Jacqueline Cochrane.
   ___ a. Jacqueline Cochrane was a famous woman pilot.
   ___ b. Jacqueline Cochrane was a famous pilot.
   ___ c. Jacqueline Cochrane is the only famous woman pilot in the U.S.
   ___ d. History has not remembered Jacqueline Cochrane.

2. She set the highest altitude record for women—48,000 feet.
   ___ a. No woman pilot flew higher than Jacqueline Cochrane.
   ___ b. Jacqueline Cochrane flew higher than other female pilots.
   ___ c. Male pilots flew faster than Jacqueline Cochrane.
   ___ d. Jacqueline Cochrane flew higher than male pilots.

3. In 1938 she won the Bendix Trophy for being the fastest pilot by flying 2,042 miles in 8 hours, 10 minutes, 31 seconds.

___ a. In 1938 Jacqueline Cochrane was the fastest female pilot.

___ b. In 1938 Jacqueline Cochrane was the fastest pilot.

___ c. The Bendix Trophy honors the fastest pilot.

___ d. Jacqueline Cochrane proved that she was the fastest pilot in 1938.

4. In 1953 she was the first woman to fly faster than the speed of sound.

___ a. Before 1953 only men flew faster than the speed of sound.

___ b. Jacqueline Cochrane is the only woman to fly faster than the speed of sound.

___ c. Before 1953 no woman flew faster than the speed of sound.

___ d. Jacqueline Cochrane never flew as fast as the speed of sound.

5. After she flew faster than the speed of sound in 1953, she became a member of the very exclusive club of people who had broken the sound barrier.

___ a. Before 1953 some people had broken the sound barrier.

___ b. In 1953 Jacqueline Cochrane became a member of a special group.

___ c. Jacqueline Cochrane was the first person to break the sound barrier.

___ d. It was in 1953 that she flew faster than the speed of sound.

6. When she flew the Sabre jet in 1953, her insurance was more expensive than she expected—$10,000 per flying hour.

___ a. Jacqueline Cochrane knew exactly how much the insurance was going to be.

___ b. Jacqueline Cochrane thought the insurance was going to be less than $10,000.

___ c. Jacqueline Cochrane knew the insurance was going to be inexpensive.

___ d. Jacqueline Cochrane thought that the price of the insurance was correct.

7. Flying planes in the 1930s was much riskier than it is today.

___ a. It's much more dangerous to fly planes today than it was in the 1930s.

___ b. It's much safer to fly planes today than it was in the 1930s.

___ c. It was not more dangerous to fly planes in the 1930s than it is today.

___ d. It was not as safe to fly planes in the 1930s as it is today.

8. She held many records, but in 1961 she held more speed records than any other pilot in the world.

___ a. In 1961, no male pilot had more speed records than she did.

___ b. In 1961, no female pilot had more speed records than she did.

___ c. Jacqueline Cochrane had many records in her lifetime, including speed records.

___ d. Jacqueline Cochrane had only speed records in 1961.

Exercise 7. **TOEFL Review**

Part 1. Completion. For items 1 through 8, circle the letter of the answer that best completes the statement or question.

1. Of all the students in class, Josie is ___ one.

   a. the goodest

   b. the best

   c. the better

   d. the good

2. I'm freezing! It's 30 degrees ___ here than it is outside.

   a. more cold

   b. the coldest

   c. more colder

   d. colder

3. Don't you think it's ___ to play sports than watch them?

   a. more interesting

   b. most interesting

   c. the more interesting

   d. the most interesting

4. How do you feel today—better? No, actually I feel ___ .

   a. the worst

   b. worse

   c. more worse

   d. worser

5. You need to drive ___ on icy roads than on dry ones.

   a. more carefullier

   b. the most carefully

   c. more carefully

   d. carefullier

6. In the U.S., domestic cars are often __ than imported cars.

   a. more cheap

   b. more cheaper

   c. cheaper

   d. more cheaply

7. Hurricane Floyd was one of __ and __ hurricanes of 1999.

   a. the more larger / most destructive

   b. the most largest / most destructive

   c. the larger / more destructive

   d. the largest / most destructive

8. Jacqueline Cochrane was the first woman to fly _____ the speed of sound.

   a. the faster than

   b. faster than

   c. faster as

   d. more fast than

Part 2. Error Identification. For items 9 through 15, read each sentence carefully. Look at the underlined parts. Circle the letter that shows the incorrect part of the sentence.

9. Matt <u>is</u> <u>more wise</u> and <u>more mature</u> <u>than</u> Pete.
       A   B   C   D

10. TOEFL exercises <u>are</u> <u>the</u> <u>most hardest</u> questions <u>to</u> answer.
                  A B   C   D

11. Amelia Earhart <u>was</u> a <u>more</u> <u>famous</u> pilot <u>to</u> Jacqueline Cochrane.
                  A   B   C   D

12. Small cars <u>are</u> usually <u>more cheaper</u> to own and operate <u>than</u> large <u>ones</u>.
             A   B   C   D

13. <u>That</u> was <u>one</u> of the <u>worse</u> movies in <u>the</u> world!
      A   B   C   D

14. The <u>more</u> <u>expensive</u> watch I own <u>is</u> also <u>the oldest</u>.
           A   B   C   D

15. I live farther <u>from</u> my parents <u>as</u> my <u>two</u> sisters <u>do</u>.
               A   B   C   D

Unit 11
Modals

Exercise 1.   **Realia** Read the following dialogue about use of the family car and underline the best modals.

Son: Dad, _____ I use the car tonight?
          (can, might)

Dad: Why do you need my car?

Son: I told my date that I _____ pick her up about 7.
                                (may, would)

Dad: If you told her that you _____ pick her up at 7, you _____
                                    (would, must)   (will, must)

78

think that I'm going to say yes. What _____ you do if I had to work

(must, would)

tonight?

Son: I guess I _____ ask one of my friends if we _____ double

(couldn't, could)   (could, will)

date with them.

Dad: I guess you _____ do that because I have to work at that time.

(should, may)

I _____ not have to work tomorrow night, so you _____ be

(might, could)   (might, can)

able to use the car then.

Son: Thanks, but I _____ not have a date tomorrow night!

(may, must)

Exercise 2.   **Original Sentence Writing**   Write four complete sentences and four complete questions using the words given. Add capital letters as needed. Be sure to add a period at the end of each statement and a question mark at the end of each question.

example: should / wear / raincoat

You should wear a raincoat in the rain.

OR   **Should you wear a raincoat today?**

1. might / leave / tomorrow

_____

2. could / give / me / address

_____

3. may / invite / me / to the prom

_____

4. will not / graduate / this year

_____

5. had better / take / medication

_____

6. must not / own / a car

_____

7. would / like / coffee

_____

8. should not / buy / expensive gift

_____

_____

Exercise 3.   **Realia** Read the following discussion of ways to save money on medications. Then circle the correct modals.

When you are not feeling well, do you go to the doctor right away? There are alternatives to paying high doctor bills. You ❶ (can, must) buy over-the-counter medication, or you ❷ (may, should) want to purchase generic drugs. You ❸ (might, can) find all these alternatives at your nearest pharmacy. First of all, you ❹ (must, should) ask the pharmacist if what you are considering has any side effects. You ❺ (could, will) also ask your doctor if any generic drugs are equal to name brand drugs that he or she has prescribed for you. You ❻ (can, might) save a lot of money by using generic drugs. So, do you think you ❼ (should, can) seek advice about other kinds of medication? What do you have to lose?

_____

Exercise 4.   **Game/Puzzle** Find and circle eight modals in the word search puzzle. The words are written horizontally, vertically, diagonally, forward, and backward. Good luck! When you have finished, write the eight words on the lines below.

```
R  Z  A  H  P  V  X  C  P
T  P  M  A  Y  W  A  O  C
H  D  N  U  O  N  I  U  L
G  H  S  U  S  Y  B  L  N
I  Y  L  T  W  T  M  D  L
M  D  S  H  O  U  L  D  B
```

_____   _____   _____   _____

_____   _____   _____   _____

Exercise 5.   **Dialogue and Conversation Practice** A grandfather and grandchild are talking. Fill in the dialogue with the correct modals.

Child: Grandpa, when you were younger, _____ you run fast?

Grandpa: Oh, yes. Long ago, I _____ run really fast.

Child: Grandpa, when you were younger, _____ you see without glasses?

Grandpa: Oh, yes. I _____ see a fox a mile away.

Child: Grandpa, when you were younger,

_____ people use

computers?

Grandpa: Oh, no. We _____ do

that. We didn't have computers.

People _____ write

things, but they used a typewriter.

Child: Wow, what's a typewriter?

Exercise 6. | **Sentence Study** | Read the beginning sentences. Then read the answer choices and put a check mark in front of **all of the sentences that are true** based on the beginning sentences. Remember that more than one answer is possible sometimes.

1. My friend is having a barbecue tomorrow night. I am on a special vegetarian diet, so maybe I should bring something that is on my diet.
   ___ a. I can't eat my friend's food.
   ___ b. I should eat my friend's barbecued food to be polite.
   ___ c. I have to avoid meat.
   ___ d. It's OK for me to eat vegetables.

2. My driver's license expired last week, so I had to take the driving test again yesterday. I wasn't able to pass it. I might try again next week.
   ___ a. My license is not current.
   ___ b. I have to pass the test before I can drive without any problems from the police.
   ___ c. I should take the test five or more times.
   ___ d. I must try again.

3. When my grandparents were young, things were a lot cheaper.
   ___ a. They could buy things for less money.
   ___ b. They had to spend more than a dollar for certain kinds of candy.
   ___ c. There is not much difference in prices then and prices now.
   ___ d. They almost never bought any candy for themselves.

4. The "Garfield" cartoon in yesterday's newspaper was very funny. You ought to read it if you have the time.
   ___ a. You must read it.
   ___ b. You have to read it.
   ___ c. You should read it.
   ___ d. You ought to read it.

5. We might go to the park on Saturday if it doesn't rain.
   ___ a. We may go to the park.
   ___ b. If it rains, we won't go.
   ___ c. It won't rain on Saturday.
   ___ d. We had better go to the park on Saturday.

6. You must know Pete; he was in high school with us.
   ___ a. Pete probably went to a different high school.
   ___ b. You and I went to the same high school.
   ___ c. Pete, you, and I went to the same high school.
   ___ d. Pete, you, and I graduated in the same year.

7. I don't have to pay the rent today.
   ___ a. I won't pay the rent today.
   ___ b. I mustn't pay the rent today.
   ___ c. I can pay the rent another day.
   ___ d. It's possible to pay the rent today.

8. Would you mind holding the door open while I bring in the groceries?
   ___ a. The groceries are not in the house.
   ___ b. The speaker needs some help.
   ___ c. The speaker wants the listener to close the door.
   ___ d. The listener is going to cook dinner soon.

Exercise 7.   **TOEFL Review**

Part 1.   Completion. For items 1 through 8, circle the letter of the answer that best completes the statement or question.

1. I ___ not be able to go to Andy's party Saturday night because my sister is not sure if she needs a babysitter that night.

   a. can

   b. should

   c. might

   d. could

2. I am a reporter from the *Times*. ___ I ask you a question?

   a. Should

   b. May

   c. Will

   d. Would

3. Michael is very strong for his age. He ___ lift the sofa without any help.

   a. would

   b. may

   c. might

   d. can

4. When my grandpa was young, he __ run in marathons.

    a. can

    b. could

    c. should

    d. will

5. If I shopped earlier, I __ avoid all the crowds.

    a. will

    b. should

    c. can

    d. could

6. If I had a car, I __ not take the bus.

    a. could

    b. should

    c. would

    d. will

7. You __ take the pan off the stove before the sauce burns.

    a. will

    b. could

    c. would

    d. had better

8. You __ use a pen. You can use a pencil.

    a. mustn't

    b. don't have to

    c. shouldn't

    d. can't

Part 2. Error Identification. For items 9 through 15, read each sentence carefully. Look at the underlined parts. Circle the letter that shows the incorrect part.

9. <u>Because</u> she <u>has</u> a bad cough, Hillary <u>will goes</u> to <u>the</u> doctor this afternoon.
     A   B   C   D

10. <u>The final</u> exam will be very difficult, <u>so</u> you <u>should to</u> <u>study</u>.
      A   B   C   D

11. Katherine <u>cannot</u> go <u>to</u> the movies with <u>us</u> last Monday or <u>last night</u>.
               A   B   C   D

12. Yesterday John wasn't <u>able do</u> his <u>homework</u> because <u>his</u> computer <u>broke</u> down.
                       A   B   C   D

13. This window <u>is really</u> hard <u>to open</u>. <u>You could</u> help me <u>open it</u>?
                A   B   C   D

14. You <u>would</u> do this before you <u>leave</u>. I <u>need</u> it for <u>today's</u> meeting.
        A   B   C   D

15. He <u>mightn't</u> be <u>able</u> to go <u>because of</u> his <u>broken</u> leg.
       A   B   C   D

Unit 12

Problem Words

Exercise 1.　**Realia**　Read the following postcard from Peter to his friend
Ahmed. Fill in the blanks with the correct forms of the choices
in parentheses.

Hi, Ahmed!

Well, here I ❶ (be, have) _____ on vacation. I ❷
(be, have) _____ so lucky! The island is ❸ (very,
too) _____ beautiful. The weather is perfect—
not ❹ (too, very) _____ hot and not ❺ (too,
very) _____ cold.　There ❻ (is, are) _____
gorgeous flowers and plants everywhere you
look.　The island ❼ (have, has) _____ brightly
colored birds and fish.　It's ❽ (too, enough)
_____ hard to describe the island in words, so
I'm taking lots of pictures.

See you soon!
Peter

Ahmed Sanjay
842 Lands Lane
Leadsville, British Columbia
CANADA

Exercise 2.　**Original Sentence Writing**

Part 1.　Describe your favorite or ideal place by finishing these sentences. Use the
words in parentheses to help you write the sentences. You may use more
than one word to complete your sentences.

1. My favorite place is _____ . (name the place or put the

location)

2. It has _____ . (noun)

3. There is _____ . (noun)

4. There are _____ . (noun)

5. It's very _____ (adjective) because

   _____ . (give a reason why)

6. It's not too _____ . (adjective)

7. It's a perfect place to _____ . (verb)

8. The two things I like best about my favorite place are

   _____ . (nouns)

Part 2. Now draw a picture of your favorite place and describe it to one of your classmates.

Exercise 3.   **Realia**   Read the following advertisement for a home security system and underline the correct words in parentheses.

How safe is your home? Call **1-800-ITS-SAFE**
❶ (to, for) find out. We can tell you if your home is protected from ❷ (almost, most) thieves and burglars.

❸ (Almost, Most) people think their homes are safe if the doors and windows are locked. This is true in ❹ (almost, most) cases, but ❺ (to, for) complete protection, you need the "Stop Thief 620."

The "Stop Thief 620" is so small it's ❻ (almost, most) undetectable. Once it's installed, you will ❼ (almost, most) forget it's there because you'll feel so much safer. ❽ (To, For) order your "Stop Thief 620" today, call **1-800-ITS-SAFE**. Install the "Stop Thief 620" ❾ (to, for) safety and protection starting tomorrow. You'll be glad you did!

Exercise 4. **Puzzle/Game** Word Bingo! Have you ever played bingo? It is a fun and exciting game of chance. Our version of bingo is called Word Bingo. To play, first you will need to prepare a game card similar to the chart shown here. Do this on a separate sheet of paper. Use the words and phrases in the two lists on the following page to fill in the blank squares. Write each of the items in the first box twice. Be sure to mix them up. Write the items in the second box once. If an item contains a word such as ADJECTIVE, NOUN, or VERB, do not supply a sample adjective, noun, or verb. Just write ADJECTIVE, NOUN, or VERB as shown. Do not write in the box marked "free space."

Have you filled in your card? If the answer is yes, then you're ready to play Word Bingo. Here are the rules.

1. Each student will need some markers (small objects such as coins). Your instructor may provide these, or you may supply them yourself. These markers will be used to cover the squares on your game card when correct answers are given. Put one marker on the square marked "free space."

2. Your instructor will have a box or another container with slips of paper. Each piece of paper will contain a word or phrase from one of the two lists.

3. Students will take turns choosing a slip of paper from the box. After choosing a slip, the student will read the word or phrase out loud and then use it in a sentence.

4. Listen to the sentence. Decide together if it is correct. If everyone agrees that the sentence is correct, take one of your markers and cover the square on your game card where the word or phrase is written. Then another student will take a turn. If the sentence is not correct, the slip of paper will be returned to the box, and another student will take a turn.

5. The first student to cover five squares in a row (horizontally, vertically, or diagonally) is the winner. You can count the "free space" square as one of the five squares if it is part of your row. Then you will only need to cover four more squares to complete the row.

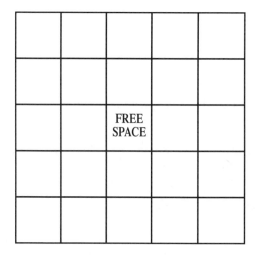

<table>
<tr><td>very</td></tr>
</table>

very	10 years old
too	hungry
there is	has
there are	have
almost + ADJECTIVE	almost + VERB
most + NOUN	there aren't
to + VERB	doesn't have
for + NOUN	most of

Exercise 5. | **Dialogue and Conversation Practice** | Work with a partner. You and your friend are trying to make some plans for the weekend. One of you wants to see the movie *Life's a Mountain.* The other wants to visit the Contemporary Art Museum in the city. Using the information provided below, create a conversation in which you discuss plans. End the conversation by deciding which activity you'll do.

Person 1

let's / movie / weekend
Life's a Mountain
there / two people / live / mountain
they / work together / survive

museum / cost / $15

Person 2

what / name / movie
what / about

sound / very / boring
I / better idea /
let's / go / museum

that / too / expensive

most paintings / too hard / understand

I / discount coupon /
it / cost / $3
that / almost free
museum / sell / book /
book / explain / everything

A: _____

_____

B: _____

_____

A: _____

_____

B: _____

_____

A: _____

_____

B: _____

_____

A: _____

_____

B: _____

_____

A: _____

_____

B: _____

_____

Exercise 6.   **Sentence Study** Read the beginning sentences. Then read the answer choices and put a check mark in front of **all of the sentences that are true** based on the beginning sentences. Remember that more than one answer is possible sometimes.

1. She almost ran off the road during the storm.
    ___ a. She had a car accident during the storm.
    ___ b. She was able to control the car during the storm.
    ___ c. The storm made it difficult to stay on the road.
    ___ d. She did not have an accident during the storm.

2. I can't believe our math teacher! He always gives very difficult tests.
    ___ a. The tests in the math class are always difficult.
    ___ b. No students ever pass the math tests.
    ___ c. Students have to study a lot to pass the math tests.
    ___ d. Our math teacher told us some lies.

3. He forgot to stop at the store for salad.
    ___ a. He doesn't remember stopping at the store to buy salad.
    ___ b. He stopped at the store but not to buy salad.
    ___ c. He didn't stop at the store to buy salad.
    ___ d. He bought several things, but he forgot to buy salad.

4. Most of the students studied for the English final.
    ___ a. All of the students studied.
    ___ b. Not more than 50% of the students studied.
    ___ c. More than 50% of the students studied.
    ___ d. Most of the students made almost perfect scores.

5. We're almost finished with this book.
    ___ a. We finished the book.
    ___ b. We will finish the book soon.
    ___ c. We will not finish the book.
    ___ d. The part of this book that we did not read is small.

6. The difference between the two banks is their interest rates.
    ___ a. The banks have different interest rates.
    ___ b. One bank has a higher interest rate than the other.
    ___ c. There is no difference between the rates.
    ___ d. We don't know which bank has a better interest rate.

7. This silver Mercedes is too expensive for us.
    ___ a. We can buy this car today.
    ___ b. We can't buy this car because it costs a lot.
    ___ c. This car costs more money than we have.
    ___ d. We don't really like this kind of car very much.

8. In all areas of the state of Florida, there are more than 160 sites of historical or cultural interest for tourists.

   ___ a. Florida has at least 160 places for tourists to visit.

   ___ b. There are historical and cultural areas throughout Florida.

   ___ c. Some of the tourists in Florida are interested in historical or cultural sites.

   ___ d. In the state of Florida, there are 160 sites of historical interest.

Exercise 7.   **TOEFL Review**

Part 1.   Completion. For items 1 through 8, circle the letter of the answer that best completes the statement.

1. ___ the answers were easy to find.

   a. Almost

   b. Most

   c. Most of

   d. Almost of

2. He studied an extra hour ___ .

   a. for pass the test

   b. to pass the test

   c. and pass the test

   d. for passed the test

3. I ___ that I can't concentrate on anything.

   a. am very hunger

   b. have so hungry

   c. am so hungry

   d. have too hungry

4. Guess what? ___ new family in our neighborhood.

   a. There is a

   b. That is a

   c. There are some

   d. Those are some

5. I didn't buy the shoes because they were __ for me.

    a. very small

    b. too much small

    c. much small

    d. too small

6. __ seven days in a week.

    a. It has

    b. There are

    c. There have

    d. It have

7. They overslept and were __ for work.

    a. late almost

    b. almost late

    c. most late

    d. the almost late

8. The reviews of that movie __ highly critical.

    a. was

    b. didn't have

    c. didn't were

    d. were

Part 2. Error Identification. For items 9 through 15, read each sentence carefully. Look at the underlined parts. Circle the letter that shows the incorrect part of the sentence.

9. <u>Almost</u> of <u>the</u> students <u>were</u> unhappy with the <u>new</u> textbooks.
    A   B   C   D

10. She <u>came</u> to <u>the</u> United States <u>for</u> learn <u>English</u>.
         A   B   C   D

11. My <u>score</u> on <u>the</u> TOEFL test <u>was</u> <u>too</u> high.
         A   B   C D

12. How <u>many</u> letters <u>have</u> <u>there</u> in the <u>English</u> alphabet?
         A   B   C   D

13. The books on the reading list was long and difficult.
    A   B   C   D

14. Last week almost of the workers put in very long hours.
    A   B   C   D

15. The children have afraid of most of the scary Halloween costumes.
           A   B   C   D

Unit 13

Review

Exercise 1. **Realia** Read the following postcard from Helga to her mother. Underline the correct articles.

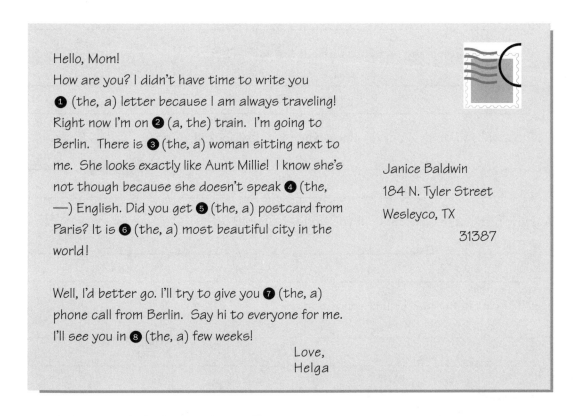

Hello, Mom!

How are you? I didn't have time to write you ❶ (the, a) letter because I am always traveling! Right now I'm on ❷ (a, the) train. I'm going to Berlin. There is ❸ (the, a) woman sitting next to me. She looks exactly like Aunt Millie! I know she's not though because she doesn't speak ❹ (the, —) English. Did you get ❺ (the, a) postcard from Paris? It is ❻ (the, a) most beautiful city in the world!

Well, I'd better go. I'll try to give you ❼ (the, a) phone call from Berlin. Say hi to everyone for me. I'll see you in ❽ (the, a) few weeks!

Love,
Helga

Janice Baldwin
184 N. Tyler Street
Wesleyco, TX
31387

Exercise 2. **Original Sentence Writing** Congratulations! You are on the last unit of the *Clear Grammar 2 Student Workbook!* Take a few minutes to think about all the grammatical structures you have practiced and learned. Then read the questions below and write your answers in complete sentences. Afterward, share your answers with your classmates and instructor.

1. What are you going to do with this book when you finish the last exercise? Why?

_____

_____

2. What will you remember most about this book? Why?

_____

_____

3. What was the most difficult structure for you to learn? Why?

_____

_____

4. What was your favorite unit? Why?

_____

_____

5. Which exercises, if any, were too difficult for you? Why?

_____

_____

6. What did you think about the book when you first looked at it?

_____

_____

7. How many of the exercises did you do in the book?

_____

_____

8. What part of the unit helped you the most?

_____

_____

Exercise 3. **Realia** You belong to the English Pen Pal Club. As a member, you receive the monthly newsletter. Read this month's newsletter and underline the correct words in parentheses.

Dear English Pen Pals!

Happy New Year! Next month ❶ (is going to be, was) a busy month for some club members. Last month pen pal members in ❷ (the, ø) Arizona ❸ (begin, began) making arrangements for the annual English Pen Pal Convention.

As you all know, our conversations are ❹ (always, seldom) lots of fun. You get to meet ❺ (other, another) members of the club. Every year the convention is ❻ (better, more better) than the year before. You ❼ (must, would) register before February 10 ❽ (for, to) attend the convention.

See you there!
Your English Pen
Pals Editor,
Darren

Penelope Bumby
681 Dawes Circle
Apartment 14B
San Mateo, CA
        61335

Exercise 4.   **Puzzle/Game** Eight groups of words are given on the right. In each group, all of the words are the same in some way; that is, they all belong to a certain category. Think about the words in each group and decide what category they belong to. Write the names of the categories on the lines on the left.

1. _____ always, sometimes, never, rarely, seldom, often

2. _____ me, us, you, him, her, them

3. _____ my car, Jean's pencil, ours, the leg of the chair

4. _____ smaller than, more quickly than, prettier than, more beautiful than, faster than

5. _____ went, cost, forgot, sang, bought, wrote

6. _____ a, an, the

7. _____ are going to, will

8. _____ may, can, would, had better, ought to

Exercise 5. **Dialogue and Conversation Practice** Work with a partner. You and your partner are the host and guest on a talk show. Today the topic is "What students can do to learn English faster." Write questions using the phrases under the "host" column. Then write answers using the list of suggestions listed under the "guest" column. Try to use as many of the words in the lists as possible in your questions and answers to create an interesting talk show discussion. You may use original questions and answers, too.

Host (questions)

how many / suggestions
can / list / some ideas or strategies
things / always / do
things / never / do
easiest / thing / learn / English
most difficult / thing / learn / English

Guest (answers)

read magazines / newspapers / books / English
write notes / messages / grocery lists / English
listen to TV / radio / music / native speakers
speak / other students / native speakers
dictionary
vocabulary flashcards
do / homework
ask questions / class
not afraid / make / mistakes

_____

_____

_____

_____

_____

_____

_____

_____

_____

_____

Exercise 6. **Sentence Study** Read the beginning sentences. Then read the answer choices and put a check mark in front of **all of the sentences that are true** based on the beginning sentences. Remember that more than one answer is possible sometimes.

1. *Andy:* I just heard that Sam won some money in the lottery. How much did he win?

   Bob: He won about three thousand dollars.

   Andy: That's great! He sure is lucky.

   Bob: Wait, that's not all; this is the second time he's won that amount.

   Andy: Wow! He's the luckiest guy I know.

   ___ a. Sam is telling Andy and Bob he just won the lottery.

   ___ b. Sam won less than seven thousand dollars.

   ___ c. Andy compared Sam's winnings to Bob's winnings.

   ___ d. Sam is the luckiest person in the world.

2. I would like to know the price of these pants.

   ___ a. I want to try them on.

   ___ b. I want to know the size.

   ___ c. I want to know about the sales people.

   ___ d. I want to know the price.

3. My car broke down, so I had to take the bus to work yesterday.

   ___ a. I usually take the bus to work.

   ___ b. I rarely take the bus to work.

   ___ c. I always take the bus to work.

   ___ d. I never take the bus to work.

4. There are six pens on the table. One of the pens is red, another is blue, others are green, and the other one is black.
    ___ a. There is more than one blue pen on the table.
    ___ b. There is one black pen on the table.
    ___ c. There are three green pens on the table.
    ___ d. There aren't any red pens on the table.

5. I need to get a library card because I need to do research about Thomas Jefferson. My history teacher often refers to him.
    ___ a. I am taking a history class.
    ___ b. Thomas Jefferson is my teacher.
    ___ c. My teacher doesn't talk about Thomas Jefferson.
    ___ d. I don't have a library card now.

6. *Mom:*   Stop this fighting right now! You children shouldn't fight over a toy. James, please give it back to your sister. And James, please ask your sister the next time you want to use her toys.
    ___ a. The toy belongs to neither child.
    ___ b. He should give her the toy.
    ___ c. He should ask her permission to use her toy.
    ___ d. Mom stopped their fighting.

7. When I am tired at the end of the week, I always take a hot bath, sometimes make a hot cup of tea, but rarely watch TV.
    ___ a. I usually go to bed.
    ___ b. I may have hot coffee.
    ___ c. I never take a shower.
    ___ d. I seldom watch TV.

8. I went to the bakery last night and couldn't make up my mind. The wheat bread smelled delicious, but the rye smelled even more delicious. However, the pumpernickel smelled the most delicious of all.
    ___ a. The wheat bread smelled as delicious as the rye.
    ___ b. The rye didn't smell as delicious as the pumpernickel.
    ___ c. The best smelling bread in the store was the pumpernickel.
    ___ d. I didn't like the wheat bread.

Exercise 7.　**TOEFL Review**

Part 1.　Completion. For items 1 through 8, circle the letter of the answer that best completes the statement or question.

1. Ursula ___ and broke her leg last week.

    a. fall down

    b. fell down

    c. fallen down

    d. falls down

2. ___ to see that person again.

    a. Never she wants

    b. She want never

    c. She never wants

    d. She never want

3. James and I live near each other. My house is on Elm street, but ___ house is on Palm Avenue.

    a. her

    b. their

    c. my

    d. his

4. ___ did you go to the mall last week?

    a. How much time

    b. How many times

    c. How times

    d. How time

5. ___ is blue.

  a. The color of the house

  b. The house's color

  c. The color house

  d. The houses' colors

6. Sharon is ___ her brother.

  a. more intelligent than

  b. intelligenter than

  c. the most intelligent than

  d. the most intelligent

7. ___ my essay and tell me what you think?

  a. Will you reads

  b. Could you read

  c. Might you reads

  d. You read

8. George is ___ to go to the beach today.

  a. very tired

  b. so tired

  c. tired very

  d. too tired

Part 2. Error Identification. For items 9 through 15, read each sentence carefully. Look at the underlined parts. Circle the letter that shows the incorrect part.

9. You <u>know</u> a lot about <u>movies</u>! <u>How often you go</u> to the <u>movies</u>?
        A   B   C   D

10. <u>I going to</u> go <u>to</u> Paris next <u>year</u> with <u>my</u> parents.
        A   B   C   D

11. We <u>bought</u> <u>the</u> new car last <u>week</u>, but it is not <u>running</u> well.
        A   B   C   D

12. Did you <u>drives</u> <u>to</u> California, or <u>did you</u> take <u>an</u> airplane?
              A   B   C   D

13. <u>Last</u> week <u>we</u> are all going <u>to go</u> to <u>the</u> graduation ceremony.
    A   B   C   D

14. <u>Can</u> I <u>helps</u> you <u>find</u> what you <u>are looking</u> for?
    A   B   C   D

15. <u>How many</u> money do you <u>have</u> in <u>your</u> wallet <u>right now</u>?
      A   B   C   D

Answer Key

Unit 1

Ex. 1, p. 1: 1. made 2. visited 3. were 4. am not planning 5. in 6. are doing 7. When

Ex. 2, p. 1: 1. Why is Linda not in school today? Or Why isn't Linda in school today? 2. Those cookies are more expensive than these cookies. 3. Jermaine lived and studied in England in 1998. 4. Right now Sally is watching television in her bedroom. 5. The students didn't (OR did not) have time to do their homework last night. 6. Why did you leave the party so early yesterday? 7. My brother doesn't (OR does not) like to play soccer, but he loves to play baseball. 8. Are you from Spain?

Ex. 3, p. 2: Answers will vary.

Ex. 4, p. 3:

Ex. 5, p. 4: Answers will vary.

Ex. 6, p. 4: 1. a 2. c 3. a 4. ad 5. ac 6. bd 7. ab 8. bd

Ex. 7, p. 6: 1. b 2. c 3. d 4. a 5. b 6. d 7. b 8. a 9. D 10. B 11. A 12. B 13. B 14. A 15. C

Unit 2

Ex. 1, p. 8: 1. an 2. a 3. Ø 4. Ø 5. an 6. Ø 7. a

Ex. 2, p. 8: 1. The Nile River is in Egypt. 2. Berlin is the new capital of Germany. 3. The Kingdom of Saudi Arabia is on the Red Sea. 4. His cousins live in Texas, Florida, and California. 5. Nepalese guides climb the Himalayan Mountains. 6. I always stay at the Hilton Hotel in New York. 7. She studies at UCLA in California. 8. Hurricanes form in the Atlantic Ocean.

Ex. 3, p. 9: a, the, Ø, the / an, the, an, the / the, Ø, the / an, a, the

Ex. 4, p. 10: 1. A, England, the 2. Ø, a, Ø, South America 3. The, Ø, Ø, Tokyo 4. The, a, Ø, Africa 5. Ø, a, the, United States 6. Ø, Ø, Lake Geneva 7. The, Ø, Russia, Ø 8. A, the, Ø, Qatar 9. Ø, Lisbon, the, Ø 10. The, Great Lakes, Ø, the 11. The, Ø, Australia, Ø 12. Ø, Abu Dhabi, the, the

Ex. 5, p. 11: Answers will vary.

Ex. 6, p. 12: 1. a 2. b 3. bcd 4. bc 5. abc 6. ab 7. d 8. cd

Ex. 7, p. 13: 1. c 2. a 3. b 4. d 5. a 6. c 7. b 8. a 9. A 10. B 11. C 12. A 13. D 14. B 15. D

Unit 3

Ex. 1, p. 16: are . . . going to live, is . . . going to be, are . . . going to have, are . . . going to retire, are . . . going to go, are . . . going to visit, are . . . going to earn, are . . . going to drive

Ex. 2, p. 16: 1. Where are you going to go next weekend? 2. Who is going to wear her new dress next Saturday? 3. What are Karen and Billy going to watch tonight? 4. When are your parents going to go to Mexico? 5. Why aren't you going to go with them? 6. Who(m) are you going to be with this weekend? 7. Where is your pet cat going to stay while you're on vacation? 8. How many countries are Ricardo and Tom going to visit?

Ex. 3, p. 17: Answers will vary. Some suggested answers are the following: 1. Nathan is going to watch a baseball game on the 14th. 2. Dee is going to be at a ballet recital on Monday the 15th at 8 p.m. 3. Mom is going to get a haircut on the 16th. 4. Dad is going to be at a seminar on the 17th. 5. The dog is going to go to the vet Thursday at noon. 6. Tina is going to be at a science fair on Friday. 7. Les is going to be at a bike show on Saturday.

Ex. 4, p. 18:

Ex. 5, p. 18: Answers will vary.

Ex. 6, p. 19: 1. cd 2. a 3. d 4. bcd 5. bc 6. b 7. abd 8. bd

Ex. 7, p. 20: 1. b 2. c 3. a 4. d 5. c 6. d 7. b 8. c 9. C 10. D 11. C 12. D 13. A 14. D 15. A

Unit 4

Ex. 1, p. 23: 1. bought 2. cost 3. saw 4. Did . . . buy 5. went 6. got 7. forgot 8. spent

Ex. 2, p. 24: 1. Did the parents understand the child's question? 2. I didn't catch a cold last month. 3. The choir sang your favorite Christmas song. 4. Didn't Mrs. Jones speak with the phone company about the problem? 5. You held your breath. 6. Your brother didn't break his leg. 7. Did your mother make dinner? 8. Didn't Mary write several letters to her pen pal?

Ex. 3, p. 24: 1. Sarah/She was free. OR She didn't (OR did not) have to do anything. 2. Sarah/She woke up at 6. 3. Sarah/She met Joe. 4. No, the president didn't (OR did not) meet Sarah at the sales meeting. The VP met her. 5. Sarah/She wrote a proposal. 6. Sarah/She left at 3. 7. Sarah/She went to night class. 8. Sarah/She wrote the final draft. OR Sarah/She gave it to the boss.

Ex. 4, p. 26:

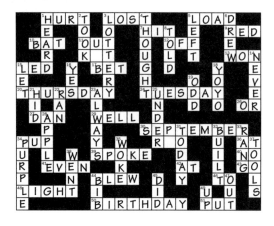

Ex. 5, p. 28: B: did . . . buy, B: didn't buy, V: forgot, did . . . buy, B: made, wrote, V: did . . . mean, B: meant

Ex. 6, p. 29: 1. bc 2. d 3. a 4. acd 5. b 6. a 7. cd 8. abc

Ex. 7, p. 30: 1. d 2. c 3. a 4. d 5. a 6. d 7. c 8. d 9. C 10. D 11. B 12. D 13. A 14. C 15. A

Unit 5

Ex. 1, p. 33: Answers will vary.

Ex. 2, p. 33: 1. How old is your car? 2. How many sisters do you have? 3. How long is one foot? 4. How often do you watch television? 5. How tall is Marcus? 6. How much money do you have (in your pocket)? 7. How many hours do you work per day? 8. How heavy was your suitcase?

Ex. 3, p. 34: Answers will vary. Some sample questions are the following: 1. How long did you study at the University of Pennsylvania? 2. Did you work during school? 3. How long did you do computer training? 4. How much professional computer experience do you have? 5. How were your grades in high school and college? 6. How many letters of recommendation did you bring?

Ex. 4, p. 35: 1. 6 2. 22 3. 20 4. 5 5. 3

Ex. 5, p. 35: Answers will vary.

Ex. 6, p. 36: 1. b 2. a 3. ad 4. ad 5. abd 6. d 7. bd 8. ad

Ex. 7, p. 37: 1. c 2. a 3. b 4. d 5. a 6. b 7. c 8. a 9. A 10. B 11. A 12. B 13. B 14. A 15. A

Unit 6

Ex. 1, p. 40: Part 1. Answers will vary. *Part 2.* Answers will vary.

Ex. 2, p. 41: 1. Steve/He always goes to the movies on Fridays. 2. Steve/He never goes to class on Thursdays. 3. Steve/He sometimes calls his mom on Sundays. 4. Steve/He seldom works on Saturdays. 5. Steve/He often does laundry on Saturdays. 6. Steve/He usually works on Tuesdays. 7. Steve/He sometimes plays soccer on Sundays. OR Sometimes Steve/he plays soccer on Sundays. OR Steve/He plays soccer on Sundays sometimes. 8. Steve/He always goes to class on Mondays and Wednesdays.

Ex. 3, p. 42: 1. Always 2. Never 3. sometimes 4. Sometimes 5. usually 6. rarely 7. often

Ex. 4, p. 42: Part 1.

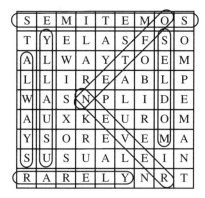

Part 2. 1. always (OR usually OR often) 2. seldom OR rarely 3. often OR usually 4. Sometimes, sometimes 5. never

Ex. 5, p. 43: Answers will vary. Suggested questions and answers: 1. How dependable are you? I'm very dependable. I'm always on time. I'm seldom sick. 2. Did you have problems with your co-workers at your last job? No, I never had problems. I always got along with people. 3. Did you ever work late? Yes, I sometimes worked late. I usually worked late when a project was due. 4. Did you attend many meetings? Yes, I did. My boss often asked me to attend meetings.

I usually wrote the minutes, and sometimes I led the meeting. 5. Are you comfortable with computers? Yes, I am. I always used computers at my last job. 6. Thank you for coming. You're welcome.

Ex. 6, p. 44: 1. c 2. ac 3. bd 4. bcd 5. ab 6. bcd 7. bc 8. bd

Ex. 7, p. 45: 1. d 2. c 3. d 4. b 5. c 6. c 7. c 8. b 9. B 10. A 11. B 12. C 13. A 14. C 15. D

Unit 7

Ex. 1, p. 48: A: my, it, me *B:* it *A:* I, my *B:* you, it, you, it *A:* it

Ex. 2, p. 49: 1. I told you/him/her/them to be quiet. 2. The eyeglasses broke when the baby threw them on the floor. 3. For Mary's birthday, her sisters bought her a watch. 4. For Peter's birthday, his brothers bought him a football. 5. My/His/Her/Our/Your/Their mother let me/him/her/us/you/them borrow her car. 6. My friends and I have similar interests. 7. Michael brought his dog to the veterinarian to give it/him/her a flea bath.

Ex. 3, p. 49: 1. I 2. it 3. them 4. their 5. them

Ex. 4, p. 50: 1. I 2. me 3. it 4. it 5. it 6. it 7. my 8. me 9. me 10. I (Answer to riddle: a grape)

Ex. 5, p. 51: O: you, me *C:* I *O:* It, its *C:* You, me, I, you, I, I, he, my, you, me, him, his *O:* You, me, it

Ex. 6, p. 52: 1. b 2. bc 3. b 4. abd 5. d 6. cd 7. ab 8. ad

Ex. 7, p. 53: 1. c 2. d 3. c 4. c 5. d 6. a 7. d 8. b 9. C 10. B 11. C 12. B 13. A 14. B 15. D

Unit 8

Ex. 1, p. 56: the others, other, other, Other, another, it, the others. Use *another* with a singular count noun. Use *other* if you have *the* or *my* or *this*. Use *other* if the noun is plural.

Ex. 2, p. 56: 1. Lisa has two cars. One is yellow, and the other is green. 2. I have three sisters. Two of my sisters are doctors. The other is a dentist. 3. Do you have a pet? No, I don't have one. 4. Shelly wants another glass of milk. 5. My CD broke yesterday. I want to buy another one. 6. There are two new pens on the table. I will take one, and you can take the other (one). 7. Do you want another piece of pizza? 8. My mother has three puppies. Two like to stay inside, and the other likes to stay outside.

Ex. 3, p. 57: 1. One 2. it 3. others 4. another 5. another 6. it 7. it 8. other two

Ex. 4, p. 58: Original sentences: Answers will vary.

Ex. 5, p. 58: Answers will vary.

Ex. 6, p. 59: 1. ab 2. c 3. ad 4. b 5. c 6. ac 7. c 8. bcd

Ex. 7, p. 60: 1. a 2. c 3. c 4. d 5. b 6. a 7. b 8. a 9. D 10. D 11. C 12. C 13. D 14. A 15. C

Unit 9

Ex. 1, p. 63: 1. Its 2. its 3. its 4. Its 5. its 6. her 7. 's (family's) 8. their 9. 's (dog's)

Ex. 2, p. 63: Answers will vary. The correct possessive forms are as follows. 1. the girls' pencils 2. the city's airport 3. the arm of the chair 4. the thickness of the book 5. yesterday's news 6. my sandwich 7. the price of the stock 8. the prime minister of Britain (OR Britain's prime minister)

Ex. 3, p. 64: 1. Debbie's school dress 2. the baby's new jumpsuit 3. the Charles family's new towel 4. Mama's nightgown 5. Dad's old jeans 6. the apartments' clothesline

Ex. 4, p. 65: my grandmother, my grandfather, my grandparents

Ex. 5, p. 65: C: of, 's (Boston's), of *C:* 's (Carphone's) *B:* his *C:* my *B:* of

Ex. 6, p. 66: 1. ab 2. ad 3. a 4. ab 5. ab 6. abcd 7. a 8. c

Ex. 7, p. 67: 1. c 2. a 3. d 4. a 5. d 6. b 7. d 8. d 9. C 10. B 11. D 12. A 13. D 14. D 15. A

Unit 10

Ex. 1, p. 70: 1. younger 2. more energetic 3. shinier 4. better 5. easier 6. faster 7. more expensive 8. happier

Ex. 2, p. 70: Answers will vary.

Ex. 3, p. 72: 1. warmer 2. bluer 3. lowest 4. most delicious 5. more crowded 6. more beautiful 7. faster 8. sooner

Ex. 4, p. 72:

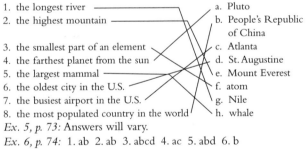

1. the longest river — g. Nile
2. the highest mountain — e. Mount Everest
3. the smallest part of an element — f. atom
4. the farthest planet from the sun — a. Pluto
5. the largest mammal — h. whale
6. the oldest city in the U.S. — d. St. Augustine
7. the busiest airport in the U.S. — c. Atlanta
8. the most populated country in the world — b. People's Republic of China

Ex. 5, p. 73: Answers will vary.

Ex. 6, p. 74: 1. ab 2. ab 3. abcd 4. ac 5. abd 6. b 7. bd 8. abc

Ex. 7, p. 76: 1. b 2. d 3. a 4. b 5. c 6. c 7. d 8. b 9. B 10. C 11. D 12. B 13. C 14. A 15. B

Unit 11

Ex. 1, p. 78: S: can *S:* would *D:* would, must, would *S:* could, could *D:* should, might, might *S:* may

Ex. 2, p. 79: Answers will vary but must include the modal.

Ex. 3, p. 80: 1. can 2. may 3. can 4. should 5. could 6. can 7. should

Ex. 4, p. 80:

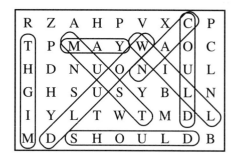

Ex. 5, p. 81: C: could G: could/was able to C: could G: could/was able to C: could G: couldn't/weren't able to, could

Ex. 6, p. 82: 1. acd 2. abd 3. a 4. cd 5. ab 6. bc 7. cd 8. ab

Ex. 7, p. 83: 1. c 2. b 3. d 4. b 5. d 6. c 7. d 8. b 9. C 10. C 11. A 12. A 13. C 14. A 15. A

Unit 12

Ex. 1, p. 86: 1. am 2. am 3. very 4. too 5. too 6. are 7. has 8. too

Ex. 2, p. 86: Part 1. Answers will vary. *Part 2.* Pictures will vary.

Ex. 3, p. 87: 1. to 2. most 3. Most 4. most 5. for 6. almost 7. almost 8. To 9. for

Ex. 4, p. 88: Answers will vary.

Ex. 5, p. 89: Answers will vary. Suggested answers: Let's go to the movies this weekend. What's the name of the movie that you want to see? It's called *Life's a Mountain.* What's it about? There are two people who live on a mountain. They work together to survive. That sounds very boring. I have a better idea. Let's go to the museum. The museum costs $15. That's too expensive. I have a discount coupon. It will cost $3. That's almost free. Most paintings are too hard to understand.

The museum sells a book. The book explains everything.

Ex. 6, p. 91: 1. bcd 2. ac 3. c 4. c 5. bd 6. abd 7. bc 8. abc

Ex. 7, p. 92: 1. c 2. b 3. c 4. a 5. d 6. b 7. b 8. d 9. A 10. C 11. D 12. B 13. C 14. B 15. A

Unit 13

Ex. 1, p. 95: 1. a 2. a 3. a 4. — 5. the 6. the 7. a 8. a

Ex. 2, p. 95: Answers will vary.

Ex. 3, p. 96: 1. is going to be 2. ∅ 3. began 4. always 5. other 6. better 7. must 8. to

Ex. 4, p. 97: 1. adverbs of frequency 2. object pronouns 3. possessives 4. comparatives 5. irregular past tense verbs 6. articles 7. future tense verbs 8. modals

Ex. 5, p. 98: Answers will vary. Suggested answers: P1: How many suggestions are there to learn English faster? P2: There are many suggestions. P1: Can you list some ideas or strategies? P2: Yes, I can. You can read magazines, newspapers, and books in English. P1: Are there some things you should always do? P2: Yes, there are. You should listen to TV or the radio every day. You must do your homework. You should ask questions in class. P1: Are there some things you must never do? P2: Yes, there are. You must try not to speak your own language. P1: What is the easiest thing to learn in English? P2: The easiest thing to learn is vocabulary. You can use vocabulary flashcards. P1: What is the most difficult thing to learn in English? P2: I think the most difficult thing to learn is not to be afraid to make mistakes.

Ex. 6, p. 99: 1. b 2. d 3. b 4. bc 5. ad 6. bcd 7. cd 8. bc

Ex. 7, p. 101: 1. b 2. c 3. d 4. b 5. a 6. a 7. b 8. d 9. C 10. A 11. B 12. A 13. A 14. B 15. A